ESSAYS ON
CHRISTIAN
COMMUNITY

ESSAYS ON
CHRISTIAN
COMMUNITY

Do Covenant
Communities have
Something to
Contribute to our
Models of Church?

BOB TEDESCO

Essays on Christian Community
Copyright © 2019 by Bob Tedesco
All rights reserved.

Published in the United States by Credo House Publishers,
a division of Credo Communications LLC, Grand Rapids, Michigan
credohousepublishers.com

ISBN: 978-1-625861-39-9

Unless otherwise noted scripture quotations are from the
Revised Standard Version of the Bible, copyright © 1946, 1952, and
1971 by the National Council of the Churches of Christ in the United
States of America. Used by permission. All rights reserved.

Cover and interior design by Nick Mulder

Printed in the United States of America
Second edition

CONTENTS

Introduction i
1. Community and the Nature of Church 1
2. Vision 9
3. The Three Greatest Needs of the Christian Church 19
4. Models of Life A 25
5. Models of Life B 33
6. Coherence: A Gift of Community 39
7. A Catholic Apologetic for Community 47
8. A Protestant Apologetic for Covenant Community 59
9. A Scriptural Apologetic for Community 65
10. Ecumenism 71
11. Covenant Christian Community 77
12. Taking a Trans-generational Approach 87
13. Freedom and Life's Plans 97
14. A Community of Disciples on Mission 103
15. The Fruit of Unity 109
16. Anticipating Purpose 119
17. Empowered to Live in Community 125
18. Closing Comments 129
19. Summary and Conclusion 131

Footnotes 133
Appendices: 135
A. Definitions 137
B. The Fruit of Unity 143
C. Some Core Principles of Discipleship 149
D. Decisions that Impact Trans-generational Vision 151
E. Covenant of the People of God 153
F. Covenant Scriptures 155
G. Resource Reading List 163
H. The People of God: A Snapshot 165

INTRODUCTION

An Orientation to this Book

This book was primarily written for members and leaders of the Sword of the Spirit and for others who may be interested in what our collective experience might have to say to the larger body of Christ. The book assumes that people have a certain familiarity with the Sword of the Spirit. I have attempted to define terms used within the Sword of the Spirit and to describe its life and mission. There may be some that I have missed, but an imaginative reader can probably figure out what I am talking about.

In almost every case, when the word "church" is used, it is intended to mean the wider body of Christ, and not a specific parish, congregation or denomination. I believe that our community history has developed into a certain kind of prophetic modeling that can make a contribution to the wider body of Christ. Due to the potential range of readers, some further introductory comments are needed. We need to examine how our community expressions got started; how they have developed; and where we are today.

Recent Church History

The past four or five decades have seen an explosion of movements and new communities. The charismatic renewal has swept through the Christian churches touching millions. The evangelical movement which preceded it impacted denominations and approaches to reform and renewal, both locally and nationally. These two powerful engines of reform have laid a foundation for a broad set of community experiments and expressions.

The bulk of this work will be focused on specific areas of importance to understanding living in Christian community.

I especially hope to deepen the understanding that supports the actions and lifestyle embraced. This is not intended to be a complete or comprehensive collection of community-oriented topics of interest. Much more can be addressed in the future. It is worth mentioning Sword of the Spirit (see description below) documents that cover some topics in greater detail:
  1) *Community Care:* how we participate and are cared for in Christian community;
  2) *Our Call:* the beginnings and some key aspects of what the Lord has called us to do and be;
  3) *The Statement of Community Order:* how communities are ordered and fit together in the Sword of the Spirit;
  4) *Our Ecumenical Approach:* how the Sword of the Spirit approaches ecumenical cooperation and relationships with church bodies.

Words of the Lord to the Broader Church

In the past one hundred years, the Lord has spoken at least three major "words" to the church. These three words have been modeled and developed in movements that have involved millions of Christians, many of them new converts. The three words that I would highlight are:
  1) Evangelical: the call to a personal encounter with Jesus Christ and a personal commitment to him.
  2) Pentecostal: the call to be baptized in the Holy Spirit and to accept the gifts of the Holy Spirit.
  3) Community: the call to committed relationships in a discipling environment that builds the Kingdom of God.

This latest word to the church, "community," has produced hundreds, perhaps thousands of communities, many of them in networks together.

All three of these words challenge the nature of the church and call it to new realities and new expressions that could further equip it to be effective in the modern world.

Sword of the Spirit

My own network, The Sword of the Spirit (SOS), is a "community of communities" that has regions all around the world: North America, Europe, Asia, South Pacific, and Ibero-Americana (Latin America, Mexico, Portugal and Spain.).

The Sword of the Spirit has grown out of several renewal movements that preceded it. As of this printing, we have over 100 communities located in 23 countries that are in various stages of commitment, and many others exploring a relationship. We have several community initiatives in formerly communist countries and the Middle East. We are ecumenical in nature and our members are from many different denominations. This ecumenical heart is one of the key works of the Lord in our midst, and it is also one of the richest fruits of our life together.

Each community has its own name and is autonomous. It is represented on the regional council by its senior coordinator. The benefits of regional and international participation are numerous, but a few should be mentioned here. First, we seek and develop together a common way of life. We benefit from elements developed in other regions and communities. Second, building community in a healthy way often exceeds the resources present locally, especially in smaller groups. We can get help at the regional level when we need it. Third, each community benefits from a "visitation" every five years. A team of experienced community leaders is assembled and they visit a local community for a 3-4 day stay. They provide the local members and leadership with an outside, objective view of how things are going. They give a report that recommends areas that could be improved with suggestions for implementation. Fourth, and finally, we benefit greatly from the regional youth program where youth from all of the communities have conferences, mission trips, and summer internships together.

With all of this said, we see ourselves as a small part of what the Lord is doing today.

Ecumenism

The Sword of the Spirit is an ecumenical network of communities. My background is Roman Catholic and much of my thinking and resources are informed from that perspective. I have tried to use sources from across the Christian traditions to serve a broader spectrum of readers. Sources are mainly scriptural, both Catholic and Protestant, but fall woefully short from the Orthodox perspective. Appendices at the back of this book offer additional resources: definitions, other tools, and examples.

Some of our local communities are all from a single church, but are supportive of the international ecumenical vision.

My local community, the People of God in Pittsburgh, Pennsylvania, is ecumenical by intention: we have a mixture of Catholic, Protestant and Free Church members.[1]

Intentions

My intentions for writing this book are: 1) to present some key lessons learned over 35 years of local community and Sword of the Spirit leadership; 2) to share scriptural references and insights about community; and 3) to identify some additional resources that others could personally research in support of the topic.[2] This book is not intended to be an official document, but a reflection on my own experiences and lessons learned. Most chapters are "stand alone" and can be read and used in discussion groups.

Dedications

To the Lord Himself, who has seen fit to grace us with his life, his presence, his energy, and his character. To my wife Bobbie, and my ten children, whose lives have all been touched and changed by the gospel and by this work of the Lord, Christian community. To Don Schwager who inspired me to write. To Jerry Munk, who helped and encouraged me through the process; and to Bill and Gudron McMillan, who worked with and improved the final manuscript. To those who helped in this project: Jerry, Bobbie, Joanie, Pattie, Dan, Dave, and all who gave input. And finally, to all of those brothers and sisters throughout the world who refuse to sit idly by and watch the Church of Christ be marginalized.

COMMUNITY AND THE NATURE OF CHURCH

Well, I certainly feel like a lightweight defending a heavyweight title! I am not a church structure expert (ecclesiologist), nor am I an ordained pastor or priest. My professional training has been in engineering, but I do have 35 years of community-building experience which includes my membership in the People of God community in Pittsburgh, Pennsylvania, USA. Over the years, I have received a lot of training in support of this work. That experience and training notwithstanding, I believe that every layman has some credible right to comment on the state of things based on his church membership and on the full responsibility of that membership. As study after study shows a decline of the influence of the church in people's lives and decisions, it is clear that we need more than just a small set of experts to give input into the nature and expressions of church. I find it at least mildly encouraging that Jesus chose his apostles from among those who were least qualified to be built into the foundation of his church, which is now in its third millennium. In light of scripture, we *all* need to question; we *all* need to contribute; we *all* need to take a concern for the life of the church. Hopefully, this effort will be a useful contribution.

New Testament "Growth Plates"

A "growth plate" is a section or location in a bone from which all future growth and development takes place. If it is removed or seriously damaged when you're young, it can freeze or inhibit further development of the size (length and thickness) of that bone. In the New Testament there are several scripture verses which are like these growth plates: sources of life for Christian life and its renewal.

One such scriptural growth plate is John 3:16:

> *"For God so loved the world that he gave his only Son, that whoever believes in him should not perish but have eternal life."*

In such a short statement, we can learn a number of key things: 1) God loves the world; 2) He sent His Son Jesus; 3) we need to believe in Jesus to have life; 4) life is everlasting (not confined to this earth); and 5) He saves us from perishing, death, and hell. This verse is seen as seminal for Christianity.

Another such growth plate is John 3:3:

> *"Truly, truly, I say to you, unless one is born anew, he cannot see the kingdom of God."*

These two scriptures could be said to be the wellspring of the evangelical movement. Indeed, they could be said to be the wellspring of Christianity.

The Great Commandments

Another New Testament growth plate is in Matthew 22; it presupposes the two already mentioned.

> *"But when the Pharisees heard that he (Jesus) had silenced the Sadducees, they came together. And one of them, a lawyer, asked him a question to test him. "Teacher, which is the great commandment in the law?" And he said to him, "You shall love the Lord your God with all your heart, and with all your soul, and with all your mind. This is the great and first commandment. And a second is like it, You shall love your neighbor as yourself. On these two commandments depend all the law and the prophets. Matthew 22:34-40*

Again, there is much to be learned from these verses: 1) the Lord is after your heart; 2) the Lord is after your mind; 3) the Lord is after your soul; 4) He can be loved by us at all three of those levels; 5) the second is "like it", which could mean that you could love your neighbor with your heart, mind, and/or soul; 6) these are commandments and therefore demand a response; and 7) "on these two depend all the law and the prophets." (Not to be taken lightly; much of the Old Testament is summarized here).

Comments

I have always been struck by number seven above: "ALL the law and the prophets." I believe Jesus is saying that all of the Old Testament is summed up in these two commandments. At the transfiguration (Matthew 17), we know that Moses and Elijah appeared with Jesus. Moses represents the law and Elijah represents the prophets. Moses and Elijah together represent the Old Testament. Jesus completes this picture as being the full manifestation of the law and the prophets. It is He who gets the Father's attention. The Father says, "This is my beloved son with whom I am well pleased. Listen to him." And what does Jesus say? "Love God...love your neighbor...on these two...depend all..." So Moses represents the law, Elijah the prophets, and Jesus the commandments of love.

Finally, these two are summaries of the two tables of the Ten Commandments. The first table (Commandments 1-3 in the Catholic tradition) has to do with how we love God; the second table (Commandments 7-10) has to do with how we love our brothers and sisters.

Relational at its Core

Christianity, at its core, is *relational*: love of God and love of neighbor. These two bring light and standards to all of the Old Testament, all of the New Testament, the Christian life, and the Christian churches. Virtually every direction and teaching of the New Testament is a reflection of our love of God and love of neighbor.

Christianity *is* doctrinal, institutional, ceremonial, etc., but at its core it is relational: the Lord and his bride.

The second...

Jesus said, "the second commandment is like the first" so church can't be *just* worship, it can't be *just* ceremony, and it can't be *just* vertical (the first commandment). It must also be horizontal (the second commandment). As modern church life becomes increasingly de-personalized or more of a "me and Jesus" experience, a progressive draining of the church's life and heart is happening. So a community that worships God is the nature of church. Not just a *worshiping* community, but a community that is relational by intention: a community that worships God together. One pastor declared that much of modern church experience is fellowshipping with the back of the head of the "brother" in the pew ahead of you!

"What ever happened to Agnes?"

Many years ago, I read an article by a Catholic bishop, "Whatever happened to Agnes?" He wrote about a personal experience that rattled him a bit. He was fully aware of his church's new emphasis on community, and he assumed that the closest thing to that was the collection of folks who attended daily morning liturgy together: a small group who saw each other each morning at Mass. One day he noticed that one of the women was missing, and had been for several days. After a few more days, he began to ask the others. Some didn't know her name. He eventually found out that she had become ill, was hospitalized and was now recuperating. He summarized his experience by questioning our understanding, our reality of community. He was clearly disappointed. He recognized that something was wrong; something was missing. He did not offer a solution. I would say that his *worshipping* community was not a *community*; it was a set of people who worshipped together but lived separate lives and separate ways of life. Any one of them might move to the other side of the state (perhaps unnoticed) and slip into a similar group (perhaps unnoticed).

Who gets to move Heather?

Another story that gets at the relational side of Christian community is that of Heather. The People of God is an ecumenical community and we have members from several denominations. Heather was a member of one of the area's "mega-churches." For a number of personal reasons (courtship, etc.) she decided to move out of one of the community "clusters" (neighborhoods) to another part of town, closer to her church, and to leave our community. When she moved, on her last day in the People of God, it was community brothers and sisters who carried the furniture, and helped to clean and prepare the old and new apartments.

This is not meant to be a criticism or observation about a particular local church as much as it is meant to be a call to the broader Christian church: we don't know how to love each other *within* the church. We leave to families the needs which are increasingly unmet at the family level. Churches usually are not organized into small groupings that promote relationships; and in some churches that *do* have small group structures, they tend to be "study" groups rather than "life" groups where we care for each other, grow in social relationships, and seek a common way of life together.

How did we get here?

How did we get from the early church model of Christianity to where we are today in the third millennium of Christianity? For both individuals and groups, the ongoing need for renewal, restoration, and reform could be a never-ending list of things that could and should work better. It's easy to criticize; it's easy for me to see where you could improve and for you to see where I could improve. For much of Christianity though, it is a "code blue"[1] situation. There are too many indicators of the declining influence of religion and the rising influence of secularism.

We see in this "snapshot" of the early church from Acts 2:42-47, that real community was put in place after Pentecost. They "spent time" together (v. 42) learning, praying, having fellowship, and having meals together. They spent time together "in their homes" (v. 46). They had committed fellowship (v. 44) and cared for one another's physical needs (v. 45). "Day by day" (v. 46) they met as a group. It wasn't just a Sunday worship community; their pattern was a life together, a life of community.

So, how did we get to where we are today, where so many Christians are looking for a minimal answer to the nature of the church? I believe the answers to that are very, very complex and have components at every level of humanity: spiritual, psychological, sociological, economic, etc. I'd like to propose a few for us to consider.

A few centuries ago, there was a certain natural community in place; many lived in villages, and towns were small. Making a living necessitated certain relational realities. People needed each other and looked out for each other. Families worked together in the family business or trade. Many villages and towns had a marketplace where people met and the church was central to community. When the Industrial Revolution took place, it set off a migration by which more and more people left rural regions to come into the bigger towns and cities. This was one beginning of a pattern that was destructive to natural community at the local level and at the family level. It was less and less the case that families worked together, or that fathers worked with their sons. Today it is common for a father to go to his job, a mother to go to her job, and the children to go off to school. These were all done together or in close proximity in earlier times.

With the growth of large cities, and the divisions and isolation of family members, we are less relational or less tied to one another. Today, it is often considered a virtue if you need no one. In past times it was a given that you needed others; life was corporate.

There are many other factors that contribute at many different levels: the isolating effects of TV, video games and modern entertainment, etc. Suffice it to say that we are very, very isolated and very, very different from the New Testament church. (Another snapshot is seen in Acts 4:32-35.)

What to do?

Again there are many and varied answers to this question. I suppose you could just say, "Try something! Try anything! And do it quickly!" We in the Sword of the Spirit are not the first to notice the serious spiritual and natural differences between New Testament and modern expressions of Christianity. Dehumanizing modern life patterns have been noticed by Christians and non-Christians alike. You have to love and appreciate those who are at least trying to make a change.

For Christian renewal and reform, we should first understand that Christianity is *relational*. It is not emphasizing independent isolation, but inter-dependent relationships. I would say churches and large Christian groups should reorganize into small groups, after identifying and training a small set of leaders who are truly converted and dedicated to Christ. Again, the small groups are "life groups" not just study groups: life is shared; some accountability is in place; a contribution to the mission is made.

Additionally, I would say, "Get help." Wading into these waters unprepared will cause unnecessary casualties. Remember this: different people have different capacities for failure. One strikeout can cause some young boys to never pick up a bat again. Others will not leave the plate until they hit the ball. Wise approaches on the part of leadership can reduce the number of casualties as we grow into a Christian family.

The rest of this book will present some elements of Christian community in an attempt to make some contributions to our understanding of the nature of church and our experience of the models of church. These elements and approaches have been developed in our life together and are, hopefully, part of the solution. But first, let's begin to close this chapter remembering these verses...

- John 3:16 tells us that God loves the world and sent his son Jesus.
- John 3:3 tells us that we can see the kingdom of God if we are born again.
- Matthew 22:37-40 tells us the laws of love.

So, it is a fact that God loves us and has sent his son to redeem us. Our initial response is to be born again. The Christian life, *our lived-out response*, is to love God and neighbor with all that we have... and that *is* the quintessential nature of church.

VISION

Introduction

In a yearly review of our community life, our coordinators recognized that certain elements of our community life had weakened or slipped a bit. We discussed the situation in ways that identified a weakening of our overall vision, and for certain elements of our way of life, a loss of vision.

Proverbs 29:18a says, "Where there is no vision the people perish." The King James Version, Darby and Amplified translations use the word "vision". But the New International Version translates the word "revelation"; and the New Life version translates the same word as "understanding". All three words offer some insight, and whether we "perish" (King James Version), "run wild" (The Living Bible), or "cast off restraint," it is clear that vision, understanding, and revelation have a lot to do with our long term health, success, and good order. We need to hear, embrace, and protect the vision over the years. We need to periodically review our call and refurbish weakening elements.

Holes...The danger of holes

If there are "holes" or missing elements in our vision, revelation, or understanding, there will be a price to pay. The Lord mercifully protects our shortages and shortcomings as we develop, but He expects us to "get it" as He reveals elements that are necessary to grow and move on.

BOB TEDESCO

As a seventeen year old, I had a 1953 Kaiser which had begun to burn oil. I decided to overhaul the engine (new rings, main bearings, rod bearings, etc.). It took longer than I thought and was a bit more expensive. Everything seemed to go well...until the last day of work, the day of "finishing touches". A friend of mine, a football player, dropped in to see if he could help a bit. I let him tighten the head bolts, according to a certain order. I was a bit preoccupied with other parts when a "crack!" broke into the normal sounds of working. This young man was so strong that he broke one of the head bolts and a job that was nearly finished was suddenly set back seriously.

Now, there are ways to remove broken bolts, but this one broke deep and between two cylinders. To make a long story longer, it could not be fixed without a major outlay of cash and time. So, I decided to put everything together and see how important this one four-and-a-half-inch bolt was. I pretended that everything was in place. It worked fine for awhile until the head gasket failed between the two cylinders. Then white smoke (water vapor) began to billow out of the tail pipe. I had always enjoyed skywriters, so I was initially amused. Driving my car became quite cumbersome with the need to add water on a regular basis. Things went downhill from there.

This single, small part in an engine weighing hundreds of pounds became increasingly problematic. Power was reduced, and the maintenance needed to keep the car running was becoming too bothersome.

So, too, with our vision, revelation, and understanding: "holes," or missing parts, can be crucial for things to work well. More experienced groups and leaders can help us to recognize and repair flaws or weakened elements in our vision. In the Sword of the Spirit communities we have "visitations" every five years where a team of leaders from other communities spends four or five days to review and make recommendations about our community life.

But, what is the vision? What is Christian community? The following section presents elements that describe our life together. It will not be as much a definition as it is a set of beliefs that reveal some descriptive elements.

The Christian ideal has not been tried and found wanting. It has been found difficult, and left untried. G.K. Chesterton

We Believe...

The following set of statements reveals not only our beliefs, but it also reveals a certain history of how the Lord has worked with us. There is a certain sequence to the revelation upon which our community life is based. Some of the elements are more certain than others, and some are more reflective of the particular call that we have in the Sword of the Spirit. These beliefs are not an official list or an "Apostle's Creed", but they do reveal a lot about who we are and what we value.

We believe in an encounter with Jesus Christ that results in a personal relationship with him. This has been the strong contribution of the evangelical movement which has breathed life into millions across all denominational lines.

We believe in the Baptism of the Spirit and the charisms. These gifts are tools for building the Body, and are not given primarily for personal edification. This Baptism in the Spirit has been the strong contribution of the Charismatic Renewal movement and it, too, has changed the lives of millions of people. Worship is life-filled and Spirit-filled as Christ ministers to His body through His disciples. We have seen what he meant when he said, "It is good for you that I go away for I will send my Spirit upon you." John 16:7 (paraphrase). We are a Pentecostal people.

We believe that scripture is the word of God. For many of us, this has been a kind of conversion. Something spiritual has happened as we have become almost supernaturally aware of the Lord speaking to us through scripture.

We believe that life should be lived according to the scriptures. Does the world need more Bible studies? Or does the world need Bible application groups where the life prescribed and described by God can be modeled for a world desperately in need of a better way? We could study difficult prophecies or mysterious scripture verses, or we could live life according to the word and the verses that we can easily understand.

We believe in ecumenism (again a "conversion" may be needed). Life on earth is to show forth the Lord's kingdom and to get us ready for heaven. In heaven there will be Catholics, Lutherans, Presbyterians, Baptists, etc. Whatever seems to divide us here, we <u>will</u> be together there.

We believe in lay leadership. One of the main results of the Charismatic Renewal has been the raising up and empowering of the laity. The job before us is too large to fall just to the ordained. The work of the apostles, pastors, prophets, evangelists, and teachers is to equip the saints for the work of ministry. (Ephesians 4:11-12)

We believe in evangelism. We can't help but tell of the wonders that Christ has done for us and his Spirit has worked in us. It is a fruit of Pentecost.

We believe in spiritual warfare. We know that we have real enemies in Satan and his fallen angels. We believe they must be resisted personally and corporately. We don't blame them for our acts or our weaknesses, but we must fight them vigorously when they attempt to exploit our flaws.

Section Review

All of the elements mentioned so far were present in the early Charismatic Renewal. Its health has been somewhat dependent on accepting and protecting these "gifts" of the Spirit. For example, to reject ecumenism is to eliminate one of the main reasons for the modern day outpouring of the Holy Spirit. It is an affront to the Lord to say, "I don't like that part!" Remember, He is getting us ready for heaven. As the various denominational expressions of the Charismatic Renewal have pulled back to "familiar" territory they have effectively eliminated one of the main works of God. This was meant to be a unifying work of God. Drawing back has led to a weakening of power, witness, and expression.

The next elements that were developed moved us beyond the Charismatic Renewal and toward the community movement.

We believe in covenant: covenant love, covenant relationships, committed relationships. When North American leadership groups began to talk about committed relationships, you could almost see the fear in our eyes. The Lord was planning to build something and as individualistic westerners we were commitment-phobic. We had quite a few independent ministries and big spirits.

We might view works of God as a three-stage rocket: The first stage has a lot of energy and makes a lot of noise, but it does not make the whole trip. Each stage is necessary. Each stage might think it's the payload, but you might find yourself discarded into the ocean. (Note #1: first stages and tanks can be reclaimed and recycled). So what is the payload? What is the

Lord really doing? What will last? (Note #2: payloads are often very small compared to the initial launch vehicle).

Covenant love is a blockbuster revelation about the nature of God and we get to model it! You may have heard the song that says, "What the world needs now is love, sweet love." What the world *really* needs now is *God's* love, covenant love, which is faithful, reliable, and steadfast love.

Too many marriages are failing, having an unraveling effect on society. If our life together did nothing more than support covenant love in marriage, our investments of time and money would be well spent and pleasing to God.

We believe that the Father wants a family…a big one. This is big; it may be the (payload) focus of everything else we can mention. I think the use of the word "family" is key. All through the New Testament we see the use of the titles "brother" and "sister" (family). We see in John 14:23 "…we (Father and Jesus) will come to him and make our home with him" (family). Romans 8:29 (New International Version) says that Jesus is the "firstborn of many brothers" (family). We are being prepared for life in the eternal family of the Father, and we would do well to prepare <u>as family</u> for that life. It's not <u>primarily</u> a battle between good and evil. It's primarily about the Father reclaiming his family through the work of Christ.

We believe that something is wrong. Movements, communities, and even church splits are signs that people are searching. This is not meant so much to be a criticism of churches and denominations, but a statement about a reality of the modern condition. It is easy to criticize, but important, more difficult, and necessary to reflect on the modern reality.

We believe that more is needed. It is probably self-evident that the existence of movements and communities reflects the belief that something more is needed.

> There are 68 million Catholics in the U.S.
>
> The Bad News:
> 8.1% to 10.1% of all Americans (as many as 38 million people) used to be Catholic, but have left the church.
>
> The Worse News:
> Only 23% of Catholic adults in the United States say they attend Mass weekly.
>
> The Worst News:
> Only 4.5% of Catholic adults in France say they attend Mass weekly.[1]
>
> The Best News:
> The Lord has a plan and He has begun to implement that plan.[2]

We believe that something more is needed in today's toxic culture. If a radical pagan religion drives out all Christians, then that culture is toxic to Christianity. Modern culture is becoming increasingly toxic and hostile to Christianity. It can't be "business as usual" for the church. If we observe the state of the Roman Catholic Church in Europe, we can see a revealing example: empty cathedrals, religion dropping in influence, and Christianity not thriving. The Holy Spirit has been responding by initiating various forms of movements and new communities. The witness and the existence of these new forms challenge the nature and the expressions of life in the Christian churches. These communities initiate and develop new forms and new approaches that complement the existing ones. These initiatives should not be just tolerated as curiosities or rejected as threats. They are, in many cases, true initiatives of the Holy Spirit and as such they should be received and celebrated as prophetic paradigms.

We believe that the Lord wants a people that He can direct. The first area affected is that of our everyday way of life. In addition to that, together we are often inspired to sponsor a certain concert, organize a week of healing services or invite and welcome some key Christian teacher. These are just examples that illustrate the many kinds of events, hospitalities, and services that our local body has sponsored over the years. This responsive and nimble "waiting for instructions" is the kind of servant-body that our local community intends to develop. This is in fact one of the prophetic paradigms mentioned earlier. It might be our group serving the national Lutheran conference, or the Presbyterian one, or receiving out-of-state visitors into our homes as their children attend our summer camp. We always saw ourselves as a relational group, but the servant-group aspect was a later understanding of our life together.

We believe in the call to discipleship. The "great commission" of Matthew 28:18-20 is often quoted in regard to evangelism but it's actually a direction with several parts:

1) *Go into all the world* (It would not be limited to Israel or nearby regions.)
2) *Baptize them* (Lead them and introduce them to the Lord.)
3) *Teaching them to observe all that I have commanded you* (It would involve formation as well as evangelism).

Discipleship is initiated by a personal decision to accept the Lord Jesus and for formation in the spiritual life and in personal character. Discipleship is *initiated* by a personal decision to accept the Lord Jesus. Discipleship is *developed* by receiving formation in the spiritual life and personal character. Discipleship is *lived out* in relationship with other Christian disciples. People sometimes do well with environmental approaches, but often wrestle with the more personal pastoral care. For us, pastoral care is defined as the care given to individuals within a small group (most often men's and women's groups) by an older or more experienced Christian brother or sister, who meets with us personally to discuss our plans and concerns, as well as to assist with our decisions and approaches to life.

A helpful example is Tiger Woods, the greatest golfer in the world. Tiger Woods has a coach! Is the coach a better golfer? No. But the coach can often see things that Tiger can't: little habits that he has developed, changes in his approach, and changes in his balance that are sapping his power. Similarly, *any* brother can be used by the Lord to help another brother. A mature brother-in-the-Lord can be even more helpful. The decision for discipleship is a lifelong one, but it changes in nature as we mature.

We believe that Christianity is relational. "And he said to him, 'You shall love the Lord your God with all your heart, with all your soul, and with all your mind. This is the great and first commandment. And a second is like it: You shall love your neighbor as yourself.'" (Matthew 22:37)

Christianity is also doctrinal, institutional, behavioral, structural, sacramental, etc. This is another prophetic paradigm being presented by the Holy Spirit. Jesus said *all* the law and *all* the prophets depend on these two: love God, and love your neighbor as yourself. If Christianity is just doctrinal, *just* institutional, etc., it runs the risk of losing its heart. When the heart is gone we lose the passion, the energy, and the commitment. The empty cathedrals are right around the corner as the next signal. Something more is needed and the Holy Spirit is revealing His answers.

We believe that covenant community is intentional relationships with the focus on building and being the kingdom of God together. Our activities and events together are designed to foster relationships.

We believe in the scriptural roles of men and women. Specifically, we emphasize that men need to step up as husbands, fathers and heads of family: to "love their wives as Christ loved the church" and to "raise their children in the discipline and instruction of the Lord." (Ephesians 5:23&25; 6:4)

We believe in family order: that the husband has a role; the wife has a role; the mother and father have a role together; and that the children are not to run the family (nor is their "schedule of activities" to dominate the family's life).

We believe that daily personal prayer is integral to our life as a body. Our relationship with the Lord has everything to do with all that we hope for, hope to build, and hope to live for. Personal prayer is where we spend time with Him, experience Him, and make sense out of our lives. Daily prayer is one of our commitments.

We believe that the Lord calls families and not just individuals into community. We call this our trans-generational call or trans-generational community. We expect to have second and third generation members...and we do. That is not to say that all of our children will join the local community, but they will have the opportunity to join. We <u>work</u> at passing on the vision to the next generations. We see the vision that the Lord has given as valuable, as life saving, and as life supporting (See chapter on Transgenerational Approach).

We believe that the familial nature of the body needs to be restored to the church of Christ. Every group that endures over decades will have institutional aspects to its life: organization, policies, etc. Those same groups will have activities that express their nature. Covenant Christian communities have distinctive organizational elements, policies and activities. But, at the most fundamental levels, we are brothers and sisters in Christ, and members of the family of God.

We believe in the bulwark being built. The Lord has told us that we are being built into a bulwark. The work has begun in us and will continue as we grow in Him. We are not just to be a shield against the toxic elements of modern culture, but we are to be an example of Christian culture that models His way of life. We are to be a network, a community of communities who live a common way of life.

We believe that we have been called and set in place by the Lord. We don't see our life together as just the actions of men and women, but as something initiated by the Lord Himself. I have heard it said that depression and despair are at epidemic levels in modern society. We believe that Christ and the way of life that He calls us into are answers to that epidemic. We personally and corporately do not have all the answers, but the Lord has answers and solutions to society's dilemmas.

THE THREE GREATEST NEEDS OF THE CHRISTIAN CHURCH

A number of years ago, a friend and co-worker came to me and said, "I need to talk to you about some serious questions that I have about the Catholic Church." Al had been listening to a televangelist who had been systematically criticizing the various denominations, and apparently it was the Catholics' turn. Al is a free-church assistant pastor with a number of Catholic friends. I was able to adequately address his concerns, and at the end of our discussion, I said, "Al, this was fun, but you have somehow missed the main issues!" He said, "Well, what are they?" My response was, "I'll never tell!"

That is the subject of this chapter...not just for Catholics, but for the Christian churches in general. It is the case that the Christian churches drift in and out of the need for reform and renewal and even restoration. Even the first century church, which gets so many positive reviews, drifted in and out of trouble.

- **Ephesus**: *"You do not love me now as you did at first."* Revelation 2:3 (Today's English Version)
- **Smyrna**: *"You are rich!"* Revelation 2:9b (Today's English Version)

- **Pergamum**: *"There are a few things that I have against you."* Revelation 2:14 (Today's English Version)
- **Thyatira**: *"But this is what I have against you."* Revelation 2:20 Today's English Version
- **Sardis**: *"I know that you have the reputation of being alive, but you are dead!"* Revelation 3:1 (Today's English Version)
- **Philadelphia**: *"Because you have kept my command to endure...I love you."* Revelation 3:10a, 9b (Today's English Version)
- **Laodicea**: *"But because you are lukewarm...You are poor, naked, and blind."* Revelation 3:16-17c (Today's English Version)

So, *five* of the seven churches mentioned needed something between renewal and restoration.

What is needed?

A group of 40-50 active Christians met to discuss and brainstorm the needs of the church in an attempt to identify the three greatest needs, and the range of input was remarkable. The activity itself assumes that one cares enough to even ask the question! It also assumes that humans might be able to discern the mind and heart of God well enough to identify the right needs. Furthermore, if you look over the Lord's complaints in Revelation, you'll see a list with some variety, some personalized or localized shortcomings.

The short list generated in this chapter is intended to be general in its observation and application. It relies heavily on scripture, as well as quotes from Baptist and Catholic Church leaders.

#1 Born Again

"I tell you the truth, unless a man is born again, he cannot see the Kingdom of God." John 3:3 (New International Version)

Billy Graham has repeated this verse thousands of times to individuals, and to crowds of thousands and tens of thousands. It is the basis of the evangelical movement; it has been the theme of countless crusades, retreats, rallies, revivals, days of renewal, Bible studies, etc.

Pope Benedict XVI describes this as "when the person is struck and opened by Christ..."[1] Archbishop Stanislaw Rylko says, "...there is always a personal encounter with Christ." He also says, "The greatest challenge facing the church (is) evangelization."[2] Bishop Cordes laments, "(many) have been sacramentalized but not evangelized." Andre Fossard exclaims, "God exists and I have experienced him!"[3]

So, many Baptist, Catholic and other Christian leaders would agree that the number one need of the Christian church is the encounter with Christ; to be struck and opened, to be born anew; and born again to a new life in Christ: *evangelism*.

#2 Discipleship/Formation

While many Christian leaders would agree on the number one need of the church, perhaps fewer would agree on my choice for number two: discipleship and formation. It is worth noting that the Billy Graham organization takes great care to ensure that new converts will be cared for locally before he agrees to do a crusade.

In speaking of the movements and new communities, Benedict XVI said, "It is their task to bring the message of Christ to the ends of the earth (Acts 1:8) and to make disciples of all men." (Matthew 28:19).[2] Bishop Rylko has said, "The first and greatest priority is, therefore, Christian formation."[3] Bishop Rylko further quotes John Paul II as equating the making of disciples with two priorities: a "solid and deep formation" and a "strong testimony."[4] "These are two areas in which the new ecclesial movements and new communities are producing stupendous fruits for the life of the church. These two groups have become true laboratories of faith and authentic schools of Christian life, holiness, and mission for thousands of Christians in every part of the World."[5]

#3 An Environment of Discipleship

Evangelism and discipleship need an environment that teaches disciples "to observe all that I have commanded you" (Matthew 28:19). This is raising the issue of how people change and grow. We need *teaching* and *instruction*, and we also need *training* in which a more experienced brother helps us to apply a principle in practice (teaching them to observe: knowing and doing).

In addition to the one-on-one training and help, we need to be immersed in an environment that models and supports the Christian life. In this environment we witness the joy and the reality of the Christian life and we "absorb" it. The body of Christ is pastoral by its nature and is a part of the pastoral care that we receive.

Finally, the environment of discipleship is also supportive to the lives of the *disciplers*. Those who teach and give pastoral care will also need support and encouragement. Too many Christian ministries focus on a single, gifted person who may be in danger of collapsing under the stress, or "burning out." In the Sword of the Spirit, our approach is more corporate and more environmental.

Covenant Love

Evangelism (conversion), discipleship (formation), and an environment of discipleship (community), are given here as the three greatest needs of the church. In my mind, a *fourth* is important: covenant (or covenant love). All great projects, achievements or civilizations are marked by serious commitment to the cause. Covenant characteristics are also noteworthy in Judeo-Christian history. In fact, before covenant was expressed in law and legal documents (deeds, etc.), it existed in the nature of God. Before there were an Old Covenant and a New Covenant, and before there was a covenant with Noah…there was a covenantal God! It is his nature to be loyal, faithful, reliable, consistent and true to his word. Commitment, it seems, does not scare him at all. He relishes it; he invites it; he models it; he initiates it.

Yet covenant, and covenant love are not frequent topics in Christian books and sermons. Why is that? Nothing is more repulsive to the flesh than being "locked in" or "decided". We would always like to be doing what we "feel like" doing. Certain lawyers make a living by getting us out of clear agreements and commitments that we have made. The best phone plans are the ones where "no commitment is necessary." After a while, we mistakenly attempt serious things (family life, starting a business, building the kingdom of God) with a "no commitment" attitude and those things are doomed to fail.

Covenant and covenant love are the glue that holds the discipleship environment together. The love of God is a constant. In desiring to be perfect as our heavenly father is perfect (Matthew 5:48), we intend to model his nature, and model his love to our brothers and sisters. We are "living stones" (1 Peter 2:5) and covenant love is the mortar that allows us to be built into a city on a hill (Matthew 5:14).

Word

God is a "man of His word." He is faithful, his word is everlasting. His word, and his approach to it, defines the divine. His word is so essential, so crucial, so defining that he named his son the "Word of God."

- *"The Word was God." John 1:1*
- *"And the Word became flesh." John 1:14*
- *"The name by which he is called is the Word of God." Revelation 19:13*
- *"There are three that bear record in heaven, the Father, the Word, and the Holy Ghost; and these three are one." 1 John 5:7*

Summary

In the Sword of the Spirit, we say we are a "community of disciples on mission." In this short descriptive phrase, we can see those first three elements. The fact that our communities have lasted over thirty-five years is at least an initial sign that the covenant love of God and the love of the brethren are in place.

This entire chapter is based on the assumption that the reader has some concern or questions about the needs of the church. Those who think everything is just fine will not be stirred by this discussion, while others may have a different list. When I first heard of the Baptism in the Spirit in 1970, I remember thinking, "I knew there was supposed to be more than what we were experiencing!" Something in me was expecting more. The scripture readings on Sundays always pointed to the hope of something more. There is more, much more, and we in the Sword of the Spirit are just scratching the surface of what the Lord has for us.

> "There is an urgent need for a strong testimony and Christian formation. What great need there is of living Christian communities! This is where the ecclesial movements and new communities appear. They are the answer which has been raised up by the power of the Holy Spirit to the dramatic challenge at the end of the millennium. You are this providential answer."[5] Pope John Paul II

MODELS OF LIFE A

Introduction

In the next two chapters we will consider models of life: some modern approaches to life, to marriage, to family life, and to the Christian life. In our regional (North American) development, we have had community leaders work on such topics as child-centered parenting, the media, raising boys to be men, single women and courtship, school choice pros and cons, etc. If you step back from these topics, it is easy to see that modern culture has approaches to these areas, and many of those approaches are at odds with the Christian life. Some approaches are even disastrous. Another aspect easily noticed is that we all have been influenced by these approaches and the world's approach is almost a "given" for many of us. Some of these approaches have only been in existence a few generations and could easily be considered a sociological experiment! Yet for many of us, they are almost a certainty in our minds. One example is the modern approach to courtship, which would seem dangerous and bizarre to most people from the early 1900's. We seem to have lost the posture of questioning the world's approach even though scripture warns us to be "...wise as serpents and innocent as doves." (Matthew 10:16)

Missing the mark

Consider the Greek word *hamartia*, used frequently in scripture and translated as "sin." It is a derivative of the word *hamartano*, which means "to miss the mark." In our efforts to live the Christian life we can get caught in certain cultural traps that cause us to lose focus and "miss the mark."

Our first introductory Sword of the Spirit course is called "Life in the Spirit" It is meant to lead people to Christ, to baptism in the Spirit, and to a fruitful life as a disciple in a mission-oriented community. In one of the earliest classes we introduce the "throne diagram:" a circle representing your life with a chair or throne in the middle. The question then posed is, "*Who* or *what* is on the throne of your life?" It could be the Lord at the center; it could be career; it could be pleasure; it could be money, etc. This is a way of examining our priorities and praying for the grace to make Christ the center of our lives, on the throne where He belongs.

After many years of pastoral work with individuals, couples and families, I have learned that it is possible for two Christ-centered people to enter into a marriage that itself is *not* Christ-centered at its core. The married couple is a new unit in the body and they need to specifically decide to center their marriage in Christ, in a way similar to what an individual would do. For example, a married couple praying together is somewhat analogous to a personal prayer time for the individual. The same is true for families: it is entirely possible that two Christ-centered parents with Christ-centered children will not necessarily create a Christ-centered family. The life style or "culture" of the family might not reflect Christianity, but might be more reflective of the world around it. The reasons for this can be many and varied. People might not *know* how to have a Christ-centered marriage or family. It might be a shortcoming of the Christian community or local church, or the individual's personal lack of understanding. Even with the availability of good pastoral and teaching resources it is possible to not have a Christ-centered marriage or family. In the tide of increasing secular cultural influences, our priorities can easily become blurred or even obstructed.

A Parenting Study

A recent sociological study of parenting among Christians in the United States, conducted by the Barna Group[1], was released in 2005. Here is a summary of the key points:

1) Christian parents are more likely to put an emphasis on seeing that their children get a good education than on seeing them enter adulthood as followers of Christ.
2) Christians in the United States do not parent much differently than the population at large.
3) Most believers fail to train their children to think or act differently enough for faith to make a difference. Statistically, gambling, excessive drinking, cohabitation, adultery, divorce and other unbiblical behaviors are just as likely among the children of Christians as non-Christian children.

If our approach to parenting, to education, to thinking and behavior is similar to the world, are we not *of* the world?

Cultural Influences

Christian parents often find themselves dealing with certain surface expressions only to realize that they have missed the effects of deeper cultural trends and concerns. Modesty is one example. If parents wait until their daughter begins to exhibit morality problems without addressing from a young age the child's need for training in modesty in speech, dress, entertainment, and music, they will be attempting to deal with only one aspect of a broader spectrum that has largely been ignored. They will be missing the fact that *something has been put in place before the problem manifested itself.*

Most of us, in fact, have been formed by our secular culture to give "conditioned responses." Sometimes we don't recognize the underlying value sets, including pressure from society and relatives, and the internal orientations that condition us for a certain response. We can be very culturally driven, and culturally responsive. We can be deceived: claiming to be, even *desiring* to be Christ-centered, but find ourselves on a path that goes far from the heart of God. We should remind ourselves that *the nature of deception is to not know that we are deceived!*

There are many things that get put into place in us by the culture. One example is *fear-based living*. This may be expressed as the fear of rejection, the fear of disease, fear of kidnapping or terrorism, to name a few. Fear sells newspapers; fear sells the six o'clock news. Therefore, in a shameless flood of fear-driving reports, the news media stirs fear in its customers. Fear is its lifeblood. (Note: all of these fears have a "normal" expression; it is the exaggerated emphasis that sells papers and hinders courageous living.)

Another cultural predisposition is the *need for approval*, which is connected to but different from the fear of rejection. We want approval from friends and relatives, preferring not to be seen as abnormal. But, if we live a Christ-centered Christian life we simply will not look normal. For many years in my family, we did not have a television. One day a friend and co-worker asked, "Bob, I've noticed that your children always win the yearly coloring competition in their age group. Why is that?" I responded, "That's easy. It's because we don't have a television!" Well, it was as if I had grown a third eye in the middle of my forehead! My co-worker was suddenly unable to focus his eyes. I caught him off guard, and he caught *me* off guard. If I had thought ahead, it would have been a great chance to testify to the Lord. Instead, it was like two football players who collide helmet to helmet. Each one wants to go to his bench, if only he knew where it was!

Some of us are driven by a competitive spirit: a drive to win (sometimes at all costs). Or, we can be influenced by the entitlement mentality, believing we "deserve" certain things as individuals and families. On a personal level we can be oriented by greed, orderliness, perfectionism, pleasure, fear, guilt, accomplishment, security, success, education, and so on.

Another way we can be influenced by the culture is in how we think about and view our spouse. Some culturally accepted models are to see your spouse as your best friend, confessor, fellow adventurer, partner, or lover. Some of these are more or less true, but if any one view gets exaggerated, it distorts the marriage relationship. None of these clearly gets at the question, "What is the purpose of marriage?" Or, "What is *God's* purpose for marriage?"

Families, too, are under cultural influences. One common model is to see the family as an island unto itself, a nuclear family, turned in on itself behind a protective wall, establishing its own ways and traditions. But, each individual family is painfully lacking in the resources necessary to have a good Christian family life. Eventually, the shortcomings will show as "stress cracks" as the family shoulders too much itself. Often this is rooted in the desire to "do it my way." Sometimes the individualistic fear of authority can have an isolating effect. Both are isolating and limiting.

Family Centers

Today's families can have all sorts of centers. You can have the missionary family, the social action family, the business-oriented family, the academic excellence family, the sports-based family. A family can be a part of a clan, part of a tribe, nuclear, or child-centered. When individuals or families become committed to these kinds of "centers," other things will naturally be pushed aside, further toward the fringes and away from the center. It may even be one or the other spouse. It may be that the church or Christian community takes on less and less importance. When those things get far enough away from the center, not much is required to cut them off. The two spouses can also drift away from each other toward different centers, different emphases, and different lives.

There are plenty of effects from all of these cultural orientations for individuals, for marriages, and for families. One obvious result is the increasing divorce rate. "She wants to live for 'A'; I want to live for 'B.' We're incompatible!" Today's approach to family life is creating a lot of ambivalence towards marriage among single men. The activity level and the full absorption into a child-centered family life of maximized potential for each child is a scary picture. From the outside there appears to be no peace, no "down time", no margin to "smell the roses" (if you could afford them). Besides the effect on single men, we also see a self-centering effect on some married men. Not knowing how to get their families on track, some married men become workaholics. There they find some approval and a measure of success from their work that they are unable to derive from their families. We have many rudderless people drifting without direction, without purpose.

The "Culture of Self"

Many of us are familiar with the clash between the culture of life and the culture of death: abortion, euthanasia, infanticide, etc. I suggest that this clash is really subordinate to, and a natural outgrowth of, the rising *culture of self*. We need to see that we are living in a culture of self whose very nature embraces its subset: the culture of death. If our enemy succeeds at transforming us into total self-centeredness, we will be perfectly conditioned and eminently qualified to spend eternity with him in his "kingdom." On the other hand, the kingdom of God, the culture of Christ, embraces life and calls us to die to self to find life.

There are other subsets or "isms". Relativism, narcissism, and hedonism describe this culture of self and are subsets of it. We can work on fighting all the "isms", but if we do not deal with the attitudes, values and desires that put us first, our fighting would be a waste of time. Our *real* war is dealing with the "me" at the center rather than Christ.

"I", "me" and "mine" at the center do not represent the approach of the Kingdom of God. Christ and his kingdom have to be at the center. If I keep pushing myself into the center, it pushes him out. He may be in some of my language or decorative art in the dining room, but he is no longer Lord of my life!

Christ-Centered Living

A personal conversion to Jesus Christ, spiritual growth and formation, being baptized in the Holy Spirit and ongoing Christ-centered decisions are needed for Christ-centered living. This is true not just for individuals, but for groupings as well. Marriages need to be centered on Christ; families need to be centered on Christ. If a family mainly pursues education or academic excellence, will it get the same result as a family centered on Christ? Once we make the decision to have our marriage and family centered on Christ and baptized in the Holy Spirit, we need to find out how to do that. It requires education, knowledge and support to avoid the secular drift to self. I am suggesting that not only individuals, but marriages, families, and communities should review our lives: take a hard look at our behavior, our practices, our priorities, and our decision making as a group, as a marriage, as a family, and as a community.

The congregation that started the WWJD (What Would Jesus Do?) movement has been a bit misrepresented. The approach was more like "We will do what Jesus would do" (WWDWJWD). That's the approach we all need to take. "I will do" and "we will do" what Jesus would do. The Lord wants Christ-centered individuals, Christ-centered families, and Christ-centered communities. And that is going to require some steps.

Christ-centered Living Questions
- What does the Lord want?
- What does the Bible say?
- What is just?
- What is right?
- What have we been told to do by the Lord and how does this decision serve that?
- Does this decision lead to more or better marriages?
- Does this decision lead to more or better families?
- Does this decision lead to more or better community?
- What puts the Lord at the center?
- What is my responsibility?
- What have I covenanted or agreed to do?

What Else Can We Do?
1) It all starts with each of us deciding and moving away from the self and back to the Lord.
2) Have a pastor or Christian leader pray with you to consecrate your self, your marriage, and your family to the Lord. (This is best done by having the prayer for individuals be distinct and preceding the prayer for the married couple and later for an entire family)
3) Read scripture...a lot, regularly. It challenges the world's input constantly. Get the children to read and memorize it. Make it a part of your mealtime prayer. Get the children to answer questions from a scriptural perspective. We should look to scripture for antidotes to the world, the flesh, and the devil, but especially the flesh. The world and the enemy have less influence over a person whose flesh is broken. Reading of scripture is a genuine defense against the flesh.
4) Do a heart check. (Note: see paragraph 2 under Missing the Mark, earlier in the chapter)
5) Always suspect the "self" when you are making decisions or desiring something. It is worth suspecting, asking ourselves: "Is this really from the Lord and is it his will for me, or is it fueled by something down inside of me that is apart from the will of God?"
6) Insist on "everything that is lovely and good" (Philippians 4:8). "Think on these things." This is to say, we should focus on contentment, beauty, and blessings, and downplay negativity and criticism.

7) Pray for protection: from ourselves being blind or selfish, for our spouses from the same blindness and selfishness, for our children, and for our community—that as a people we would not be selfish in our orientation.
8) Rekindle fear of the Lord. If you distort or exclude any aspect of God's nature, you get a distorted view of who God is. An over-emphasis on God's mercy while under-emphasizing his justice will lead to an unbalanced perspective. Sin has consequences. We need to learn that and to teach it to our children.
9) Foster the corporate life beyond the nuclear family. A self-centered nuclear family can be just a group expression of the selfish individual.
10) If needed, get prayer for deliverance at the individual, marriage, and family levels.
11) Live life in a way that adds up to something.

Summary

"You are truly my disciples if you live as I tell you to, and you will know the truth and the truth will set you free" (John 8:31-32 Living Bible).

Let us not forget the beginning of the sentence. Jesus is saying, "Live in my Word, live what I have taught you, *then* the truth will set you free." It is a promise of freedom and it is worth celebrating. If we live according to his plan, and raise our children according to his plan, we will see the fruit of the Christian life and the power of the Holy Spirit revealed!

MODELS OF LIFE B

In the last chapter we briefly mentioned a few models of life, some cultural influences and the consecration of smaller groupings to Christ-centered living. Here we want to consider a bit more the issue of child-centered parenting, more on the Barna study, some results of the nuclear family model, and some "if – then" scriptures.

"Who Wants to Raise an Idiot?"

A number of years ago, Larry Badaczewski posed this question during a family teaching session.[1] No one raised their hand. He needed to explain. Fr. Richard Rohr had explained in an earlier talk[2] that Greek society had a clear emphasis on building a great city or a great state. They intentionally emphasized the corporate family and each individual made this venture a priority in the use of their skills, talents and resources. The Greek word for someone who had no concern for anything but his private life was *idiot*. The root of the word is *idios* [3, 4] meaning *"one's own."* So it's my world over everything else.

The first section of the Ten Commandments begins with our relationship with God. The second section deals with our relationships with others. The second section begins with "Honor your father and mother." It begins there, I believe, because we begin life as a child, with parents. We are prepared for life in the family and wider society *by our parents*. So children are to be raised with a concern for others: their rights and their needs. If we raise our children to be only or mainly concerned for themselves, we have raised them to be idiots and they are not prepared for the gospel or the Kingdom of God. Child-centered parenting is idiotic parenting. When we raise our children to be good members of a Christian community we will continually be presenting chances to make our plans second to the corporate needs of the body and to our mission. "I'll be missing the first half of the Steelers game because we have a gathering." Further, if your family has no concern beyond itself, you are an idiotic family.

A Parenting Study [5]

More on the 2005 Barna Group study of parenting (comparing the goals of born-again parents to the population at large):
1) That their children get a good education (39%).
2) Helping children to feel loved (24%).
3) Enabling a meaningful relationship with Jesus (22%).
4) Other desirable outcomes:
- Fostering a sense of security (16%);
- Helping them feel affirmed and encouraged (14%);
- Providing a firm spiritual foundation (13%);
- Helping them feel happy (10%).

5) Establishing appropriate moral values (4%).
6) Only three in ten included the salvation of the child in a list of parental emphases.
7) Most parents take a laissez-faire attitude to monitoring media.
8) Two-to-one measure success by "having done the best you could."
9) Less than 60% of born-again parents teach moral absolutes.

Stepping back from the Barna Study

This list of observations, when combined with those from model A, cries out for a response from Christian leaders, pastors and teachers. "Business as usual" where we study and enjoy theology, give pleasing sermons, and create mission statements is not equipping parents for the task of raising children. Whole generations are being lost or are being formed in underlying value sets that do not lay the right foundation for successful Christian living, for Christian marriages, and for authentic Christian mission. "If you love me, you will keep my commandments." (John 14:15)

A life that is oriented toward self can never please God. A life that is oriented toward self can never even understand the demands, the instructions, and the responses to the gospel. Jesus will pass through our children's lives unnoticed, inconsequential, ineffective and unappreciated.

> *"'Truly, truly I say to you, before Abraham was, I am.' So they took up stones to throw at him; but Jesus hid himself and went out of the temple." John 8:58-59*

Some Fallout of the Nuclear Family

So while the Barna study leads us to question the style, the goal and the values of modern Christian parenting, I would also like to question or challenge the framework and the expression of the modern nuclear family. I believe that we unwittingly fall into "doing" family the way those around us do it. Also, we seemed to be programmed or of a predisposition that follows those around us rather than the family that we were raised in. Additionally, if our parents were frugal and simple in lifestyle, then we may feel driven to give our children what we didn't get.

As an eighth grade boy, I was allowed to attend my first Holy Name Society meeting. Father Oliveri spoke to the men about spoiling their children. He said, "You seem determined to give them everything that you did not have. Why? Did you turn out so badly?" It never occurs to us that our parents may have <u>purposely</u> withheld things from us as a part of our preparation to be adults. For most of us, if we can't sacrifice, we will find it difficult to have children; or, we will have far fewer children than we could have had with a simpler life.

The modern nuclear family then seems determined to break ties with the prior generation, and that is one drawback of the modern approach: everyone starts over; everyone "re-invents" the wheel; few are wise enough to stand on the shoulders of those who have gone before them. A downstream effect of this is that the older generations are seen as less valuable, less needed, less wise, less respected, and less important. Let us call this the "marginalization of the elders."

There is often a corresponding geographic isolation of the nuclear family as we pursue careers and school systems, etc. Too many children today grow up too far from uncles, aunts, cousins, and grandparents.

These and other shortcomings of the modern approach result in a certain cultural incoherence. Our societal forms and expressions are transient. It is as if we live in motels: we are in one place with one grouping for awhile and then we move on, not unlike military family life. We do not build clans and tribes as did the peoples of times gone by. We are familial road shows, societal carnies.*

The truth is: a family needs other families, a man needs other men, a woman needs other women, and we need the older generations. No matter how much Hollywood continues to assault family Thanksgiving dinners and Christmas dinners, we need our extended family, we need others...much more than we need Hollywood.

"If-then" Scriptures: Man's Part/God's Part

As a young man, I had the privilege of giving weekly Christian instruction to high school students. By then I had come to realize that every adult and young adult needed more than Christian ideas and Christian practices...we need a personal relationship with Jesus and that relationship brings life and energy to all the rest. In any case, I was always looking for ways to use the week's lesson to challenge my young students to give their lives to the Lord.

At the time, I was actively involved in writing computer programs to solve engineering problems. While faith is very much a matter of the heart and soul, it is also a matter of the mind. I realized that these computer programs run tests as a part of their decision-making process, and the decisions to move along in the program. I decided to use this flow chart reasoning to get my students to begin to address some of the more significant spiritual questions. In such a flow chart, each line is numbered and each line has one or two operations to perform or questions to answer. For example: line 20 might be a test: "**If** X is greater than 407 **then** go to line 50". If the test is not met (X is less than 407), then you fall through to the next step (line 21).

In my evangelism flow chart there would be tests such as "Is the Bible the word of God?" If your answer was, "Yes", then the next question would be, "Do you believe that Jesus is the Son of God?" The whole exercise was meant to track your faith: to see where you are, to see where you are stuck (if that is so), and finally to come to the Lord. (Someday!)

For our purposes here, it is worth noting that *some scriptures follow this "If...Then" pattern* and it sometimes also shows as a "man's part...God's part" statement. Some might use words such as "unless" and "cannot," but the meaning is the same: *there is a requirement or a test that is followed by a response or a result.*

Some examples: (words inside parentheses are not in the verse; italics are also mine)
1) Hebrews 3:15: "If today you hear his voice, (*then*) harden not your heart."
2) John 3:3: "Truly, truly, I say to you, unless one is born anew, (*then*) he cannot see the kingdom of God."
3) John 8:51: "Truly, truly, I say to you if anyone keeps my word, (*then*) he will never see death."
4) John 9:31: We know that God does not listen to sinners, but if anyone is a worshiper of God and does his will, (*then*) God listens to him.
5) John 10:9: "I am the door; if anyone enters by me, (*then*) he will be saved, and will go in and out and find pasture."
6) John 11:40: Jesus said to her, "Did I not tell you that if you would believe, (*then*) you would see the glory of God?"
7) John 12:24, 26: "Truly, truly, I say to you, unless a grain of wheat falls into the earth and dies, it remains alone; but if it dies, (*then*) it bears much fruit…If anyone serves me, (*then*) he must follow me, and where I am, there my servant shall be also; if anyone serves me, (*then*) the Father will honor him."
8) John 13:14: "If I then, your Lord and Teacher, have washed your feet, (*then*) you also ought to wash one another's feet."
9) John 13:35: "By this (*then*) all men will know that you are my disciples, if you have love for one another."
10) John 14:14: "If you ask anything in my name, (*then*) I will do it."
11) John 14:23: Jesus answered him, "If a man loves me, (*then*) he will keep my word, and my Father will love him and we will come to him and make our home with him."
12) John 15:7: "If you abide in me, and my words abide in you, ask whatever you will, and (*then*) it shall be done for you."

13) John 15:10-11: "If you keep my commandments, *(then)* you will abide in my love, just as I have kept my Father's commandments and abide in his love. These things I have spoken to you, that my joy may be in you, and that your joy may be full."
14) John 15:14: "You are *(then)* my friends if you do what I command you."

Some Comments

1) We often expect something to happen, yet we have not done our part.
2) We are culturally conditioned to expect the best without giving the best that we have...often without giving much at all.
3) If we live according to his plan and raise our children according to his plan, we will see the fruit of the Christian life and the power of the Baptism in the Spirit revealed.

What to do?

1) <u>Hope</u> (if...then) a lot of things point to trouble, yet many point to hope.
2) The Lord is sovereign and can overcome these dangerous trends in the world.
3) Starting with us: suspect the self.
4) Identify plans, hopes, dreams and intentions that limit the Lord.

* "carnies:" carnival workers, vagabonds, traveling independent workers.

COHERENCE:
A GIFT OF COMMUNITY

In recent decades and certainly through the twentieth century, society has changed significantly in structure. When the world changes, people change, and the Christian church is changed as well. In the past thirty to forty years, we have seen the Lord responding to those changes and restoring something *ancient*.

If we look at Old Testament societies, we can see individuals, couples, families, clans* (two or more generations), tribes, and a people. Within the "people" we can see other groupings: priestly, governing, military, workers, etc. Modern societal structure (especially western societies) seems to look more like: individuals, couples, families, weak extended families, and nations. Life is lived and decisions are made in a way that repeatedly destroys connectedness until we are isolated units. In our Sword of the Spirit communities we see individuals, couples, families, clans, the local community, a region and an international community of communities (a people).

Two Founding Directions

In the summer of 1973, our local community was given two founding words: "Gather my people together;" and "Build to last."** We have responded to the first word (gather) with numerous expressions of evangelistic outreach: Life in the Spirit courses, retreats, conferences, concerts, prayer meetings, men's breakfasts, etc. We have also repeatedly emphasized evangelism on a personal level. "Gathering" has always been a significant part of our life together.

We have also taken "building" seriously from the beginning, and our national and international ties have had a lot to do with our understanding of how things go together in a way that will last: locally, trans-locally and internationally.

Gathering and building are expressed very well in Mt. 28:18-20, the *Great Commission*. We noticed that it says "go and make disciples...teaching them to observe *all that I have commanded you.*"

So, for us it meant first of all discipleship; a discipleship where we are formed in Christian character. Second, it meant being put together (built) in a way that can endure in a culture that is hostile to Christianity and even more hostile to Christian culture.

Our coordinators take a concern for: 1) our ongoing relationship with Jesus; 2) our underlying attitudes, postures and influences; and 3) our long-term evangelism and growth. In Acts 2:41, we see the Bible takes a concern for growth when it says "that day 3,000 were added to their number."

Community growth for us comes from adult evangelism and trans-generational evangelism (the term we use to describe our children growing into adult members of the community).

A Community of Disciples on Mission

We are a community of individuals, couples, clans and movements on mission. We have a lot of teaching material on discipleship, on community, on marriage and family life. We have very little teaching on movements and no teaching on life in a clan. We have recently developed a series on senior life, which can improve the role of seniors in community and extended families. But, we have very little written about extended family life in a Christian community.

Terminology

By "family" here, we mean the nuclear model with one generation of adults. "Clan" is used for extended family with two or three generations of adults living community life. By "movements" we mean groupings of adults with a common activity and outreach that support the overall mission of the community. Individuals and families are limited by life spans, but they lay a foundation for clans, movements, communities and the Sword of the Spirit that transcends lifetimes. Pastoral leaders and youth workers working with second and third generations have a special responsibility to be aware of and support those second and third generation members. They are key links in a network of relationships that span multiple generations.

On Mission

It is not my intention here to talk at length about our mission but it should be said that our mission is:
- To evangelize, and to lead people into real decisions to accept Jesus Christ as their personal Lord and Savior, and to baptized in the Holy Spirit;
- To lead the individuals who have made those decisions into discipleship relationships of formation in Christian character and Christian community;
- To rediscover and establish the Christian culture in scriptural wisdom;
- To establish movements and outreaches that serve the Lord's purposes.

A Bigger Vision

Our vision is often *much* too small. The Lord's plan for individuals, couples and families far surpasses our limited view and ideas. The American nuclear family model is *not* the Lord's plan. The "nuclearization" of the family is creating walled-off social units that cannot be easily accessed by other extended family members and friends. What used to be a very permeable border is becoming increasingly opaque to outside light and influence. Some of that "thickening of the membrane" is due to fear, and part of it is due to the real need to survive in a toxic culture.

We also quickly absorb other modern attitudes and approaches. "I'm eighteen and I can do what I want!" Can you pay your own bills? I knew a man who used to say, "I can't wait until my kids graduate from high school so I can send them off to college!" I had serious news for him that some of the most difficult and needy years for some children are the years between eighteen and twenty-five!

Sometimes we say, "I want the best of everything for my children." Won't they end up being spoiled "brats" if they too easily get the best of everything? Christian parents might say, "If he would only answer an altar call..." but, would he not also need discipleship, supportive relationships, and Christian character formation? "They need to maximize their gifts and potential" is also a common posture.

The Lord is saying, "Come and go with me. It will cost you, but it will be better!" The Lord has a *big* strategy for families, clans, and movements; but modern influences and limitations are blocking the next levels from developing. These influences and limitations are worst at the personal and family levels.

A Big Strategy for Clans and Movements

First, we need to say again that the Lord's plan for family is bigger than the nuclear model. Keeping that in mind, we can begin to explore what He has in mind for clans and multi-generational family life. In some of our communities we have begun to see the unfolding of these expressions as multi-generational families emerge in communities that are 30-40 years in existence. Knowing that multigenerational families are a part of His plan can sharpen the focus of my service, and my decisions can be made in light of His strategy. That is, we can live life *intentionally* and coherently to support the new life that is emerging. This is not rocket science. It is the Lord restoring and rebuilding what has been damaged or destroyed by ungodly modern living. Living for self is self-destructive at every level of life and every level of basic human groupings.

On a worldwide basis, we see a steady stream of church movements that have served to bring individuals to encounter the living Christ so that lives, families, and vocations can be restored to Him. All of this spiritual activity and energy is ultimately intended for the rebuilding of *His* family.

Again, knowing more of His plan sharpens the focus of my service: I know how to pastor or to steward that which I have been placed over. I even know more about how to write my will!

However, a greater body of teaching is still needed since the Lord is restoring expressions of the Body that we had not anticipated. For example, men and women living "single for the Lord" in an ecumenical setting and yet attached or related to a wider body of families and singles. Additionally, the fostering and protecting of clans is an area in need of teaching and development. Clusters or intentional neighborhood living has been explored with some success, but it has not yet seen the development and understanding of its dynamic to get the most out of it. But, think about that: intentional Christian neighborhoods! These would be neighborhoods where our young people could at least have some chance of developing life-long Christian relationships.

Coherence: A Gift of Community

So, all the various aspects of our life together—relationships, covenant, discipleship, mission, worship, etc.—are all meant to go together, to add up to something, to build something that lasts for God. His plan is *coherent*: it makes sense; it is understandable (though not fully revealed); it is seamless; it is discernable and intelligent; it is comprehensive; and it is long-term. We think in terms of one or two generations. He sees many. This plan involves individuals, families, clans, movements, and tribes or communities. Our lives and the lives of these groupings are meant to add up to something, to be built into something. In building terms we are not just raw materials, we are stones built into a dwelling place. In farming terms we are not just seeds of wheat scattered in a random field, but the field is prepared, turned over with the rows such that the plants support each other when the wind blows, and at the harvest, the fruit is easily gathered. *We are not a single stalk of wheat in a windstorm, but a field of wheat in mutual support.*

Life was more naturally coherent in earlier times. Farms served villages and the marketplace provided a continual intersection for people who would know each other for lifetimes. Congregations and denominations never had to take a concern for the disintegration of what seemed to be the natural structure of humanity. Today's lifestyle seems more like a patchwork of temporary relationships: in many cases functional relationships (e.g. career) which vaporize with the next downsizing, or graduation, or the next "opportunity." The Lord is restoring something in covenant Christian community: a stable network of brothers and sisters with whom we can grow old, while serving Him over the span of generations; a place where our children can grow up with friends, marry and raise their children in the company of lifelong friendships. We need to see the vision, embrace it and teach it to our children.

Coherent or "Buffet"

We are modern, informed consumers. We shop for the best: the best values, investments, groups, and activities. Often, however, we do that without a coherent strategy, or without a long-term sense of how our choices fit together. If we took a patchwork approach to planning for retirement, we would find ourselves relying on Social Security. Yet, we can invest a lot of time and money in Christianity without taking concern for how it might all fit together in the Lord's plan. Parents taking a real concern for their children often "shop" for the best schools, the best youth groups, etc. This "patchwork" Christianity does not *build* the Body of Christ, but repeatedly weakens it. In worst cases, the children are even leading the family in several directions that end up having a *disconnecting*, incoherent effect on the family. Mission trips, youth groups, retreats, gatherings, campus groups, small groups and relationships should all connect, they should build into something.

Summary

I would advise young families to plan to be a clan: to take a coherent approach to life and choices, and to raise the children so that they understand and can embrace the call. Additionally, we need to orient the family and clan beyond itself so that it embraces and is built into the wider community and even to the community of communities (the Sword of the Spirit).

More developed families will find it harder since the children will not have seen this from an early age, but we can still aid the process by making good decisions. For example, if we decide to send them to the "best" college hundreds of miles away, we made a decision that "disconnects" them from family and friends and usually results in them settling in some other area of the planet.

Mature families and singles can also live so as to support this work of God in service and in pastoral work.

> *Then I saw a new heaven and a new earth; for the first heaven and the first earth had passed away; and the sea was no more. And I saw the holy city, new Jerusalem, coming down out of heaven from God, prepared as a bride adorned*

for her husband, and I heard a loud voice from the throne saying, "Behold the dwelling of God is with men. He will dwell with them, and they shall be his people, and God himself will be with them; he will wipe away every tear from their eyes, and death shall be no more, neither shall there be mourning nor crying nor pain any more, for the former things have passed away." And he who sat upon the throne said, "Behold, I make all things new. Revelation 21:1-5

In the Spirit he carried me away to a great, high mountain, and showed me the holy city Jerusalem coming down out of heaven from God, having the glory of God, its radiance like a most rare jewel, like a jasper, clear as crystal. It had a great high wall, with twelve gates, and at the gates twelve angels, and on the gates the names of the twelve tribes of the sons of Israel were inscribed; on the three east gates, on the three north gates, on the south three gates, and on the west three gates. And the wall of the city had twelve foundations, and on them the twelve names of the twelve apostles… Revelation 21:10-14

The Lord is building something; it has a design; it has foundations, walls and gates, and a detailed plan.

"Save yourselves from this crooked generation." So those who received his word were baptized, and there were added that day about three thousand souls. And they devoted themselves to the apostles' teaching and fellowship, to the breaking of the bread and the prayers. And fear came upon every soul; and many wonders and signs were done through the apostles. And all who believed were together and had all things in common; and they sold their possessions and goods and distributed them to all, as any had need. And day by day, attending the temple together and breaking bread in their homes, they partook of food with glad and generous hearts, praising God and having favor with all the people. And the Lord added to their number day by day those who were being saved.
Acts 2:40b-47

They lived differently: not just a little differently but radically different lives. They spent a lot of time together and shared things. Their life together was a part of the Lord's plan to save them from a "crooked generation" (vs. 40).

For all of us, our lives are called to have purpose, to make sense, to add up to something; we need to stay together and make decisions and investments of time and money that support our call.

* "Clans" not used here in the negative sense.
** Prophetic direction for the People of God in Pittsburgh

CATHOLIC APOLOGETIC FOR COMMUNITY

Introduction

The next three chapters will be a focused apologetic for community: one is from a Catholic perspective, one is from a Protestant perspective, and one is from a scriptural perspective. The approaches are different. Taken together they represent and appeal to different kinds of authority that might be helpful to different readers. (Note: the Fruit of Unity chapter is a different sort of apologetic).

Two Broad Structures of the Catholic Church

The Catholic Church can be seen as divided into two types of membership—two expressions of life. The lay or diocesan structure is by far the largest and includes families and singles in local parishes under a bishop. The religious order side of things includes priests, brothers and sisters. The parallel to a bishop would be an Abbot, and an Abbess or Mother Superior would oversee the women's orders.

Religious orders have certain similarities to the new communities: they take vows, we have covenants; they have novitiates, we have formation and discipleship; they have certain accountability and spiritual direction and we have pastoral care;

they tend to have a very high degree of common life and we strive for a high degree of common life with families and singles maintaining a high degree of personal responsibility. (Note: several networks of communities have brotherhoods which are even more similar to religious orders). The similarities mentioned are notable but they do have distinct differences, especially with the degree of shared life.

The Witness of Canonizations

The largest number of canonized saints, (perhaps 10 or 20 to 1), come from the smallest structure (much smaller religious order side). So the Catholic measure of success would seem to say that vows (commitment), formation, accountability and common life have produced a high degree of recognizable holiness. Similarly, there is something about the community/formation model that works better for lay people, as a complement to parish life by orders of magnitude.

We could stop here! The witness of history for Catholics has overwhelming evidence for the community/formation model.

Quotes from Modern Documents and Presentations

We will draw quotes from two sources: "The Theological Locus of Ecclesial Movements"[2] (shown as **TL** in the footnotes and "On Ecclesial Movements and New Communities: the Response of the Holy Spirit to Today's Challenge of Evangelization"[1] (shown as "**M**" in the footnotes).

"**TL**" is a paper by Cardinal Joseph Ratzinger (now Pope Benedict XVI), and "**M**" is by Archbishop (now Cardinal) Stanislaw Rylko, president of the Pontifical Council for the Laity (the largest part of the Catholic Church mentioned earlier. These two apply mainly to Catholic movements and new communities, but they have certain implications for ecumenical communities, especially for the Catholics involved in such movements and communities. The quotes have some phrases in italics or with underlining. These do not appear in the original text, but have been added to link them to the topic. Italicized text and added "******" are inserted to highlight or give emphasis to a point. They do not appear in the original text.

We'll consider these papers in regard to some topics common

to the new communities; some quotes apply to more than one area and may be repeated. I have not added much commentary since I believe that the quotes have more power if not obscured by extra reflection on my part. While most of the quotes are encouraging to communities and movements, it is worth mentioning that almost all of these kinds of addresses by church officials have some statements of caution and concern that enthusiasm and energy do not become divisive. Local church authority and membership are worthy of respect through the process of renewal.

Encounter with Christ and Baptism in the Spirit

- "Only when the person is *struck and opened up by Christ* ...can true community grow."[2] Pope Benedict XVI
- "The Spirit cannot be correctly understood without Christ, but it is equally impossible to understand Christ without the Holy Spirit."[2] Pope Benedict XVI
- "Thus, social service is always connected in one form or another with evangelization. All of this presupposes - and the source is usually the flame of the initial charism – a deep encounter with Christ. The formation and up-building of community does not exclude the personal element, but calls for it. Only when the person is *struck and opened up by Christ* in his inmost depth can the other also be inwardly touched, can there be reconciliation in the Holy Spirit, can true community grow."[2] Pope Benedict XVI
- "…there is always *a personal encounter with Christ.*"[1] Cardinal Rylko
- "'Come and see'…There is always a 'before' and 'after' in the lives of those who belong to ecclesial movements and communities. For some, the conversion of heart is often a gradual process which takes time. For others, the conversion is an unexpected and all-encompassing 'lightning bolt' experience."[1] Cardinal Rylko
- "How many members of movements and new communities can repeat the words of convert Andre' Fossard: 'God exists, and I have experienced Him'."[1] Cardinal Rylko

Discipleship/Formation

- "It is their task to bring the message of Christ 'to the ends of the earth' (Acts 1:8 RSV) and to make disciples of all men"

- (Mt. 28:19).[2] Pope Benedict XVI
- "Above all, communion must not be conceived as if the avoidance of conflict were the highest pastoral value. Faith is always a sword, too, and it can demand precisely conflict for the sake of truth and love." (cf. Mt.10:34)[2] Pope Benedict XVI
- ** "Here the Pope notes two fundamental priorities of evangelization, of 'making disciples' of Jesus Christ today: a 'solid and deep formation' and a 'strong testimony'. These two areas in which the new ecclesial movements and new communities are producing stupendous fruits for the life of the Church. These groups have become true 'laboratories of faith' and authentic schools of Christian life, holiness, and mission for thousands of Christians in every part of the world."[1] Cardinal Rylko
- ** *"The first and greatest priority is, therefore, Christian formation."*[1] Cardinal Rylko
- ** "The Christian family is no longer capable of passing on the faith to the next generation, and neither is the parish, even though it continues to be the indispensable structure for the Church's pastoral mission in any given place."[1] Cardinal Rylko
- "And what is the motivation behind the pedagogical strength? The 'secret', so to speak, is found in the charisms which have produced them and which constitute their very soul. It is the charism which produces the 'spiritual affinity between individuals' animating a community and movement."[1] Pope John Paul II
- "The charism is also the source of the extraordinary educating power of the movements and new communities. Here I refer to *a formation whose departure point is a deep conversion of heart.* It is no accident that these new ecclesial realities include converts, people who 'come from afar.'"[1] Cardinal Rylko
- "...a distinct, specific pedagogical approach which is typically Christ-centered...It develops within Christian communities."[1] Cardinal Rylko
- "...these new movements and communities are true schools for the formation of Christian 'adults'. As Cardinal Joseph Ratzinger wrote some years ago, they are 'forceful ways of living the faith that stimulate individuals, giving them joy and

vitality; their faith really means something for the world.'"[1] Pope Benedict XVI
- "Movements know how to awaken a desire to 'make disciples' of Jesus Christ, a desire that often moves individuals, married couples, and even entire families to leave everything in order to embrace the mission...new communities are responding to *one of the most urgent needs of the Church today, which is the catechesis of adults...*"[1] Cardinal Rylko
- "...it is truly surprising to witness the missionary vision which the Holy Spirit has raised up today by means of these new charisms. The movements and new communities have become true missionary 'schools' for so many lay..."[1] Cardinal Rylko

Authority
- "...God continually stirs up prophetic men (they can be lay persons or religious, but also bishops and priests) who proclaim to it the right word that is not pronounced with sufficient force in the normal course of the 'institution.'"[2] Pope Benedict XVI
- "...his move...supplements the fatherhood of bishops and priests by the power of a wholly pneumatic life."[2] Pope Benedict XVI
- "...movements generally come from a charismatic leader and they take shape in concrete communities that live the whole gospel anew from the origin and recognize the Church without hesitation as the ground of their life, without which they could not exist."[2] Pope Benedict XVI
- "Above all, communion must not be conceived as if the avoidance of conflict were the highest pastoral value. Faith is always a sword, too, and it can demand precisely conflict for the sake of truth and love." (cf. Mt.10:34)[2] Pope Benedict XVI

Community
- "Only when the person is struck and opened by Christ...can true community grow."[2] Pope Benedict XVI
- "The same Gribomont sees the monastic community that Basil founded as a 'small group for the vitalization of the whole' and does not hesitate 'to call (Basil) the patron...of the

- new communities without vows.'"[2] Pope Benedict XVI
- "Augustine, for example, designed his whole rule ultimately on the basis of Acts 4:32: 'they were one heart and soul.'"[2] Pope Benedict XVI
- "...movements generally come from a charismatic leader and they take shape in concrete communities that live the whole gospel anew from the origin and recognize the Church without hesitation as the ground of their life, without which they could not exist."[2] Pope Benedict XVI
- "Therefore, there is an urgent need for a strong testimony and a Christian formation. *What great need there is of living Christian communities!* This is where the ecclesial movements and new communities appear. They are the answer which has been raised up by the power of the Holy Spirit to this dramatic challenge at the end of the millennium. *You are this providential answer.*"[1] Pope John Paul II
- "And what is the motivation behind the pedagogical strength? The 'secret', so to speak, is found in the charisms which have produced them and which constitute their very soul. It is the charism which produces the 'spiritual affinity between individuals' animating a community and movement."[1] Pope John Paul II

Encouragements

- ** "When these movements...are welcomed by bishops and priests...they represent a true gift of God... *I therefore recommend that they be spread and that they be used to give fresh energy...*"[2] Pope John Paul II
- "In situations of scarcity, the Church must create stopgap structures.... In general the Church must keep the number of self-created administrative structures as small as possible. It must not over institutionalize itself, but must always remain open to the Lord's unforeseen, unplanned calls."[2] Pope Benedict XVI
- "...the Church is also criss-crossed by successive waves of new movements, which re-invigorate...also serve the spiritual vitality and truth of the local churches."[2] Pope Benedict XVI
- * "Two of the constitutive elements of the reality of 'movements' clearly emerge from all this:

a) The papacy did not create the movements, but it did become the principal reference-point in the structure of the Church, their ecclesial support...The Bishop of Rome...his office...has...an apostolic character."[2] Pope Benedict XVI
- ** "...from the second century on, when the universal ministries were coming to an end, the papal claim to exercise this aspect of apostolic mission begins to be heard more clearly. It is no chance, then, that the movements, which go beyond the scope and structure of the local church, always go hand in hand with the papacy."[2] Pope Benedict XVI
- "There must also always, be in the Church, ministries and missions that are not tied to the local church alone, but serve *universal mission* and the spreading of the gospel. The pope has to rely on these ministries, they on him, and the collaboration between the two kinds of ministries completes the symphony for the Church's life."[2] Pope Benedict XVI
- "...I must say quite clearly here that the apostolic movements appear in ever new forms throughout history necessarily, because they are *the Holy Spirit's answer to the changing situations in which the Church lives.*"[2] Pope Benedict XVI
- "It is all the more true that movements cannot be organized and planned by authority. They must be given, and they are given. ...we must learn, using the gift of discernment, to accept what is right while overcoming what is unhelpful. One looking back at the history of the Church will be able to observe with gratitude that it has managed, time and again, in spite of all difficulties, to make room for the great new awakenings."[2] Pope Benedict XVI
- "...they are a gift to, and in, the whole of the Church, and must submit themselves to the demands of this totality in order to be true to their own essence. But the local churches, too, even the bishops, must be reminded to avoid making an ideal of uniformity in pastoral organization and planning.[2] Pope Benedict XVI
- "Primacy and episcopacy, the local ecclesial system and

movements need each other."[2] Pope Benedict XVI
- "Thanks to the ecclesiology and the theology of the laity developed by the Council, many groups referred to today as 'ecclesial movements' or 'new communities' have appeared alongside the traditional associations."[1] Pope John Paul II
- ** "One of the Spirit's gifts to our time is truly the flourishing of the ecclesial movements which, from the beginning of my pontificate, *I have seen and continue to see as a reason for the hope for the Church and for society*". The Pope was deeply convinced that these ecclesial movements were a manifestation of a "new missionary advent", of a great "Christian springtime..."[1] Pope John Paul II
- "Movements know how to awaken a desire to 'make disciples' of Jesus Christ, a desire that often moves individuals, married couples, and even entire families to leave everything in order to embrace the mission...new communities are responding to one of the most urgent needs of the Church today, which is the catechesis of adults..."[1] Cardinal Rylko
- "As we have seen, *the ecclesial movements and communities are truly a 'providential gift' of God to the Church*, a gift that should be received with a living sense of gratitude and responsibility..."[1] Cardinal Rylko
- "...the Holy Father *insisted* that Pastors, bishops and parish priests ought to welcome these groups 'cordially,' recognizing and respecting their particular charisms..."[1] Cardinal Rylko
- "One notes that something new is beginning: Here Christianity appears as a new reality, and is perceived as a way to live - to be able to live - in today's world by people who have often come from afar. Today there are 'isolated' Christians at the margins of our strange understanding of modernity who are willing to try new ways of living. *While they may not get much attention from public opinion, their way undoubtedly points to the way of the future.*"[1] Pope Benedict XVI
- ** "According to the then *Cardinal Ratzinger, the ecclesial movements and new communities provide something new which makes them a type of prophecy for the future.*"[1] Cardinal Rylko

- "The Church must value these realities while guiding them with pastoral wisdom, so that the Churches and the *movements are not separate realities, but rather both constitute the living structure of the Church.*"[1] Pope John Paul II

Evangelism
- "It is their task to bring the message of Christ 'to the ends of the earth' (Acts 1:8 RSV)...and to make disciples of all men" (Mt. 28:19)[2] Pope Benedict XVI
- "...Francis of Assisi and Dominic...wanted simply ...to renew the Church with the Gospel. And the very fact of being evangelists made it necessary to *go beyond the borders of Christendom*, to bring the gospel to the ends of the earth."[2] Pope Benedict XVI
- "Apostolic life calls for apostolic activity: pride of place is given, again in different ways, to the proclamation of the gospel as a missionary element."[2] Pope Benedict XVI
- "The greatest challenge facing the Church... evangelization."[1] Cardinal Rylko
- "As we have seen, *the ecclesial movements and communities are truly a 'providential gift' of God to the Church*, a gift that should be received with a living sense of gratitude and responsibility..."[1] Cardinal Rylko
- "We must reflect seriously on how we might carry out a true evangelization today...People don't know God, they don't know Christ...paganism is present." [2] Pope Benedict XVI
- "The ecclesial movements and new communities contain a precious evangelizing potential urgently needed by the Church today. Yet their richness has not yet been fully recognized or valued."[1] Cardinal Rylko
- "The movements and new communities respond to a second urgent need of great...importance, which is the need for 'strong testimony.' All Christian formation ought to have a missionary element...Missionary outreach helps baptized persons to discover the fullness of their own vocation; it helps them overcome the temptation of egoistic selfishness and the subtle danger of seeing the movement or community as a refuge or a way to flee the problems of the world in an environment of warm

friendship."[1] Cardinal Rylko
- "...is the indisputable ability to awaken the apostolic enthusiasm and missionary courage of the laity. They know how to draw out the spiritual potential of the laity by helping them smash the barriers of timidity..."[1] Cardinal Rylko

Other Comments

- "...our question: How do we characterize the relationship between the permanent pattern of Church order and ever new charismatic eruptions?"[2] Pope Benedict XVI
- ** "Basil, like today's movements, was obliged to accept the fact that the movement to follow Christ radically cannot be completely merged with the local Church."[2] Pope Benedict XVI
- ** "Christ lives, and He sends from the Father the Holy Spirit - that is the joyful and life-giving experience that is ours precisely in the encounter with the ecclesial movements."[2] Pope Benedict XVI

These two papers reveal the high level of enthusiasm and expectations that the movements and new communities have generated in high places in the Catholic Church Three popes and quite a number of cardinals and bishops have spoken of the hope that these new works of the Spirit have generated. They have seen the chance for error, yet they have also seen the chance for new life, new responses of faith in the modern world.

Conclusions

First, we saw that the historical Catholic process of recognizing holiness has leaned heavily toward those who have lived their lives in more community-like environments.

Second, we saw that the very existence of the new communities and some of their important elements are approved and appreciated at the highest leadership levels.

Finally, many Catholics have as their own experience that

of having been greatly trained, formed, and blest by some of those living within a religious order. Modern life, however, is not contributing many to the religious orders which are now, and have been for quite some time, in a state of declining membership.

It should not come as a major surprise, then, that the Holy Spirit is raising up lay communities, and that many Catholics have a predisposition to understand and respond to that initiative.

A PROTESTANT APOLOGETIC FOR COVENANT COMMUNITY

At the 2006 North American Sword of the Spirit Summer Conference, we presented three workshops intending to lay out apologetic approaches and resources for Protestants, Roman Catholic and Orthodox traditions. We drew from scripture, articles, papal encyclicals, and speeches and papers of respected church leaders. Here we will draw on resources by Paul C. Dinolfo, Ralph D. Winter, R. Pierce Beaver, Carl W. Wilson, and sacred scripture.

Difficulties Due to Range

The wide variations among Protestants present a challenge to creating an apologetic that would be helpful and accepted across the spectrum.

The primary categories of Protestants are[1]:
1) Mainline (or historic) vs. Evangelical
2) Liturgical vs. Non-liturgical
3) Presbyterian vs. Congregational

The church affiliations of Christians in the USA are[1]:
1) Catholics   24.5%
2) Baptists   16.3%
3) Methodist/Wesleyan   6.8%
4) Lutheran   4.6%
5) Presbyterian   2.7%
6) Pentecostal/Charismatic   2.6%
7) Episcopal   1.7%

The percentage of Americans who attend church during a given week are[1]:
1) Catholics   6.2%
2) Evangelicals   9.2%
3) Mainline   3.2%

Therefore our first contribution to an apologetic would be to again say, "Things are not working so well; maybe this would be a good time for someone or some set of people to try something else or something additional." Secondly, it would be a good time to expect that the Holy Spirit would be at work addressing our needs, our concerns, our weaknesses, and our lack.

Scripture and History

Another approach would be to step back to take a broad look at the New Testament church and compare that to what has happened through the ages. It can easily be seen in the New Testament that the broad-based church had stable local churches and missionary groups that evangelized; explored new prospective locations; founded new churches; and served, refreshed, and renewed existing churches. That broad-based pattern has continued throughout Christian history in both Catholic and Protestant streams of Christianity.

Warp and Woof

The church is often compared to a tapestry, which is first of all a cloth. Ralph D. Winter and R. Pierce Beaver describe the "warp and woof"[2] of Christianity with the warp being the stationary threads while the woof are the moving threads on the spindle. Both are needed: the stationary (local church) and the moving (renewal movements, communities, mission bands); both are needed for church maintenance and church growth.

Sociology Intersects Ecclesiology

In Ralph D Winters, "The Two Structures of God's Redemptive Mission", he describes the stationary part (local church body) as the "modality." The moving or missionary part of the New Testament church he describes as a "sodality." A *modality* is the normal expression of a grouping, its commonly understood pattern. A *sodality* is a somewhat specialized grouping or association. It is voluntary, and might have a narrower mission or responsibility.[2] Today's renewal movements and new communities are presented as *sodalities* and not as *modalities* or replacements for the local church.

Methodism

Wesley saw his movement as a sodality and did not intend to form a new church. He felt forced out of the Anglican Church and Methodism followed (a modality). This history points to the need for getting these distinctions clear: 1) sodalities, when welcomed and embraced, can bring evangelism, service, and refreshment to the local church; 2) when misunderstood or rejected, sodalities can result in division and separation, or, at the very least, disappointment and marginalization of gifted brothers and sisters.

Further Distinctions of Warp and Woof

As already mentioned, modalities are the stationary aspect of church. They handle the wearing task of everyday life; they care for the children; there is a sort of "structural" fellowship; and there is no distinction of age or gender. Sodalities are moving, responsive, nimble. They often have two purposes: 1) internal church renewal, and 2) outreach or mission. They *may* be limited by age, gender or marital status. They thrive on zeal and enthusiasm and are often more engaging of the young. They are "not your father's Oldsmobile" (to use a marketing phrase). A "*second decision*" or additional commitment is required (beyond modality membership).[2]

A Historic Sketch

In overview we can see these structures present throughout Christian history, and there is some advantage to looking for their different expressions. It seems likely that the Holy Spirit has initiated, inspired, and influenced these different structures to meet the needs and challenges of the peoples and various periods of history.

New Testament Church

As the first Christians were Jews, their modality was the temple and all that was familiar to them. They met together in the temple, and had meals together in their homes (see Acts 2:46). Peter and John (after Pentecost) prayed in the temple (see Acts 3:1). In the shadow of Pentecost, new things began to happen: miracles (Acts 3:7), meals together, proclaiming God's message with boldness (Acts 4:31), and sharing possessions (Acts 4:32). These were quickly followed by persecution (Acts 5:18) and martyrdom (Acts 7:58). This remarkable mix of spiritual events and inter-modal pressure and rejection was instrumental in laying the groundwork for the sodality that would develop. The new Christians were scattered far and wide (Acts 8:4). We then see the selection of Saul by the Lord himself (Acts 9:15). For his protection Saul was sent to Tarsus via Caesarea, and he later returned (Acts 12:25) with Barnabas and John Mark. In Acts 13:2, we see the Pauline mission sodality being prophetically initiated and empowered by the Holy Spirit as he says, "Set apart for me Barnabas and Saul, to do the work to which I have called them." They traveled to Cyprus (Salamis), Perga, Antioch, and Iconium, preaching and teaching in synagogues along the way. "In each church they appointed elders and with prayer and fasting they commended them to the Lord in whom they had put their trust." (Acts 14:23 Today's English Version) By this time, the pattern, the work, and the effects of this missionary sodality are well established: *it is in service to the local bodies that they are being established in each locale.*

From Then Until Now

Both structures have continued to develop and adapt with the modality being more stable than the sodality, which has had many forms. Even after the Reformation, the modality for some Protestants had a diocesan structure. In his "Structures" paper,

Winter points out that "the greatest error of the Reformation" was to reject the sodalities of their age: the religious orders. By the nineteenth century, however, Protestants were actively engaged in missions. All through the founding, settling, and evangelism of North America, we have seen the sodalities repeating the New Testament pattern: setting up local churches, establishing them, and then reaching out to new population centers. It is this last step (reaching out) that is so crucial to the ongoing growth, vitality and purpose of the modalities. It could be said that our modalities (parishes, congregations) would be much healthier if they saw themselves as "beachheads" from which further ground should be taken. It is the settled-in, coasting mentality that is so lethal to our faith. Our faith must be allowed to grow beyond its boarders or something starts to die. It cannot just be enjoyed; it must be employed, or deployed to use a military term.

Today

In these times, we have multiple examples of sodalities impacting the Protestant world and local congregations: The Billy Graham organization, Campus Crusade, Athletes in Action, Promise Keepers, InterVarsity Fellowship, the Charismatic Renewal, and the new communities (many of which are covenant communities). The new communities (and their networks) are probably more comparable to the sodalities that existed after the early church and up to the Reformation. They exist, not as in competition with, but as a support to the local congregations. They offer some hope and some promise in extending our borders, spreading the gospel, and deepening our commitment to the Christian way of life. They are a part of us. They are a gift from God.

A SCRIPTURAL APOLOGETIC FOR COMMUNITY

This chapter will gather together a set of scriptures that should be a resource for those who want to present, defend or understand the modern re-emergence of lay Christian communities. Some are used and explained in other chapters, but are also given here due to their importance. Also worth mentioning is the fact that some scriptures speak directly to the issue while others imply or suggest community as an expression of church. I would suggest that much of the New Testament seems to be addressing people (churches) whose way of life seems far different from the modern experience of church for most Christians.

One Question

At the core of much of this work is this question: "What level of relationship should members of a church expect and pursue?" There are also corresponding questions such as:

1) What does the Lord expect the church to look like?
2) How did we get to the modern approach?
3) How can we recover what has been lost?
4) How do families adjust to fit into a community-oriented church?

5) What elements of the sodality are to be experienced at the level of the modality, the local church?"

The questions can be too numerous and overwhelming, but our hope here is to explore the area from a scriptural perspective, and dig into the issue of how deeply should we form Christian relationships.

My mother used to tell me, "Blood is thicker than water." Occasionally, I would respond something like, "We are bound together by the blood of Christ which far surpasses any human family!" My mother never did join our Christian community, but she lived long enough to receive elder care far beyond anything that the family could (or would) do for her. While her mind was still working, she came to understand and expressed her appreciation for the community.

(Note: I do appreciate the role of immediate family in caring for aging or dying members; I appreciate the special bond of the immediate family as well.)

Scriptures

Familial

"*If a man loves me, he will keep my word, and my Father will love him, and we will come to him and make our home with him.*" *John 14:23* (Note: The Father and Jesus make their home with those who keep the word of Jesus. It starts here: the Father makes his home with us; his people are therefore his family and in family together.)

"*...for you know how, like a father with his children, we exhorted each one of you and encouraged you and charged you to lead a life worthy of God, who calls you into his own kingdom and glory.*" *1 Thessalonians 2:11*

"*For whoever does the will of my Father in heaven is my brother, and sister, and mother.*" *Matthew 12:50*

"*Do not rebuke an older man but exhort him as you would a father; treat younger men like brothers, older women like mothers, younger women like sisters, in all purity.*" *1 Timothy 5:1-2* (Note: "brothers," "brethren," and "sisters" are used 311 times in the New Testament referring to the Body of Christ)

Beyond Family

"For if you love those who love you, what reward have you? Do not even the tax collectors do the same?" Matthew 5:46

Community

The high degree of common life of the church at Jerusalem does not seem to be replicated in other New Testament churches, but it is worth noticing it as a "reaching for heaven". The classic descriptions of the first church are in Acts 2 and 4.

"And they devoted themselves to the apostles' teaching and fellowship, to the breaking of bread and the prayers. And fear came upon every soul; and many wonders and signs were done through the apostles. And all who believed were together and had all things in common; and they sold their possessions and goods and distributed them to all, as any had need. And day by day, attending the temple together and breaking bread in their homes, they partook of food with glad and generous hearts, praising God and having favor with all the people. And the Lord added to their number day by day those who were being saved." Acts 2:42-47

"Now the company of those who believed were of one heart and soul, and no one said that any of the things which he possessed was his own, but they had everything in common. And with great power the apostles gave their testimony to the resurrection of the Lord Jesus, and great grace was upon them all. There was not a needy person among them, for as many as were possessors of lands or houses sold them, and brought the proceeds of what was sold and laid it at the apostles' feet; and distribution was made to each as any had need." Acts 2:32-35

Trans-local Sharing

"...but that as a matter of equality your abundance at the present time should supply their want, so that their abundance may supply your want, that there may be equality. As it was written, "He who gathered much had nothing over, and he who gathered little had no lack." 2 Corinthians 8:14-15

Unity

"I do not pray for these only, but also for those who believe in me through their word, that they may all be one; even as thou, Father, art in me, and

I in thee, that they also may be in us, so that the world may believe that thou hast sent me. The glory which thou hast given me I have given to them, that they may be one, even as we are one, I in them and thou in me, that they may become perfectly one, so that the world may know that thou hast sent me and hast loved them even as thou hast loved me."John 17:20-23

"Only let your manner of life be worthy of the gospel of Christ, so that whether I come and see you or am absent, I may hear of you that you stand firm in one spirit, with one mind striving side by side for the faith of the gospel..." Philippians 1:27

Connected in Relationship
"Rather, speaking the truth in love, we are to grow up in every way into him who is the head, into Christ, from whom the whole body, joined and knit together by every joint with which it is supplied, when each part is working properly, makes bodily growth and up builds itself in love." Ephesians 4:15-16 (Note: "joints" connect, support, and nurture—when each part is working properly.)

Committed, Loving Relationships
"A new commandment I give to you, that you love one another; even as I have loved you, that you also love one another. By this all men will know that you are my disciples, if you have love for one another." John 13:34-35

"This is my commandment, that you love one another as I have loved you. Greater love has no man than this, that a man lay down his life for his friends. You are my friends if you do what I command you." John 15:12-14
"This I command you, to love one another." John 15:17

A People
"When one of you has a grievance against a brother, does he dare go to law before the unrighteous instead of the saints? Do you not know that the saints will judge the world? And if the world is to be judged by you, are you incompetent to try trivial cases? Do you not know that we are to judge angels? How much more, matters pertaining to this life! If then you have such cases, why do you lay them before those who are least esteemed by the church? I say this to your shame. Can it be that there is no man among you

wise enough to decide between members of the brotherhood, but brother goes to law against brother, and that before unbelievers?" 1 Corinthians 6:1-6* (Notes: 1. If two men had a fender bender in the parking lot of a church, would they expect the pastor to resolve their present conflict? Any conflict? 2. Most communities do not exercise this kind of responsibility. 3. Something unusual is implied: that the body of Christ can have the wisdom and authority to resolve significant conflicts between members.)

"And he said to him, 'You shall love the Lord your God with all your heart, and with all your soul, and with all your mind. This is the great and first commandment. And a second is like it, You shall love your neighbor as yourself. On these two commandments depend all the law and the prophets.'" Matthew 22:37-40 (Note: When this was given, the word "neighbor" would not have included everyone in the sense of the whole world of gentiles and pagans; it would have referred to another Jew, one of God's people.)

"But you are a chosen race, a royal priesthood, a holy nation, God's own people, that you may declare the wonderful deeds of him who called you out of darkness into his marvelous light". 1 Peter 2:9

Love in "Real Time"

"We know that we have passed out of death into life, because we love the brethren. He who does not love remains in death. Anyone who hates his brother is a murderer, and you know that no murderer has eternal life abiding in him. By this we know love, that he laid down his life for us; and <u>we ought to lay down our lives for the brethren</u>." 1 John 3:14-18

"We love, because he first loved us. If anyone says, 'I love God,' and hates his brother, he is a liar; <u>for he who does not love his brother whom he has seen, cannot love God whom he has not seen</u>. And this commandment we have from him, that he who loves God should love his brother also." 1 John 4:19-21

Be Ready

"Let your speech always be gracious, seasoned with salt, so that you may know how you ought to answer everyone. Colossians 4:6

These and many other scriptures indicate that life in the Lord's family is meant to be far more substantial than is the experience of most. For those interested, some of these verses are expanded and more fully explained in other chapters.

ECUMENISM

- We were created by the Lord for the Lord.
- We will spend eternity in heaven.
- Catholics, Protestants and Orthodox will be in heaven.
- Our lives on earth should prepare us for heaven.
- Therefore, ecumenical prayer, service, and cooperation prepare us for heaven.

The logic above can easily be dismissed as the simplistic exercise of the mind of an engineer. Certainly the logic is incomplete. There are other important reasons for ecumenical cooperation. When all of the dust settles and all of the protests have been presented, it remains an outrageous scandal that many Catholics, Protestants, and Orthodox still avoid each other like the plague. It is a scandal to the gospel and an insult to Jesus' prayer for unity. Even in settings that hope to be or claim to be ecumenical, there is often a smugness that blocks Christian brotherhood. "Are you saved?" or "How can you be in that church and be saved?" are questions that sometimes surface in ecumenical settings.

The Witness of Pentecost

The first experience of Pentecost was that of Jews from many places and of many languages who were surprised to hear their native language being spoken (Acts 2:8). Then, at the house of Cornelius, another Pentecost happens as the Gentiles receive the Holy Spirit (Acts 10:44). The Jewish believers were "amazed" (vs.

45). Peter, recognizing the Holy Spirit in them, ordered them to be baptized (vs. 48). Finally, in Acts 15, we have some Jews teaching, "You cannot be saved unless you are circumcised..." (Acts 15:1 Today's English Version). Another "ecumenical" crisis threatening the work of the gospel; another distinctive taking center stage; another competing viewpoint being presented as essential; another "ecumenical" challenge. Fortunately the early church dealt with its Jewish/Gentile challenges, although it had some setbacks.

Next, we will look at some Catholic, Orthodox and Evangelical statements.

Catholic Sources
Ut Unum Sint1 Pope John Paul II
Chapter 1: The Catholic Church's Commitment to Ecumenism

Section 20: "Thus it is absolutely clear that ecumenism, the movement promoting Christian unity, is not just some sort of appendix which is added to the Church's traditional activity. Rather, ecumenism is an organic part of her life and work, and consequently must pervade all that she is and does."

"What unites is much greater than what divides us." Pope John Paul XXIII

"When brothers and sisters who are not in perfect communion with one another come together to pray, the Second Vatican Council defines their prayer as the soul of the whole ecumenical movement."

Section 22: "If Christians, despite their divisions, can grow ever more united in common prayer around Christ, they will grow in awareness of how little divides them in comparison to what unites them."

Section 40: "Relations between Christians are not aimed merely at mutual knowledge, common prayer and dialogue. They presuppose, and from now on, call for every possible form of practical cooperation at all levels: pastoral, cultural and social, as well as that of witnessing to the gospel message.

This cooperation based on our common faith is not only filled with fraternal communion, but is a manifestation of Christ himself.

In the eyes of the world, cooperation among Christians becomes a form of common Christian witness and a means of evangelization which benefits all involved."

Chapter III: Quanta Est Nobis Via
Section 85: "In spite of fragmentation, which is an evil from which we need to be healed, there has resulted a kind of rich bestowal of grace which is meant to embellish the koinonia...**He is with us.**"

John Paul II January 22, 2003
"In fact, the present division constitutes a 'scandal' for the world and 'harm' for the preaching of the Gospel."

"The Catholic Church is "irrevocably" committed to the ecumenical way and the full unity of Christians."[2]

"This commitment is decisive for two fundamental reasons: on the one hand, unity expresses fidelity to the Gospel; on the other, as the Lord himself has indicated, it is a condition in order that all will believe that He is the one sent by the Father."[2]

Cardinal Kasper, Pontifical Council for Promoting Christian Unity January 22, 2003
"This journey of rapprochement, as the Holy Father has confirmed many times, is irreversible. It was traced for us by Christ Himself who, on the eve of His death, prayed so that all would be one. Unity is, therefore, the testament left by our Lord."

Pope Benedict XVI January 25, 2007
"Ecumenism is a deep dialogical experience; it is listening and talking to one another, knowing each better. It is a task that everyone can accomplish, especially in terms of spiritual ecumenism based on prayer and sharing that are now possible between Christians. I hope that the yearning for unity, translated into prayer and fraternal collaboration to alleviate man's suffering, can spread more and more at the parish level as well as in Church movements and religious institutions."[2]

Common Declaration of Pope John Paul II and Ecumenical Patriarch Bartholomew I
4. "In this perspective we urge our faithful, Catholics and Orthodox, to reinforce the spirit of brotherhood which stems from the one Baptism and from participation in the sacramental life. In the course of history and in the more recent past, there

have been attacks and acts of oppression on both sides. As we prepare, on this occasion, to ask the Lord for his great mercy, we invite all to forgive one another and to express a firm will that a new relationship of brotherhood and active collaboration will be established.

Such a spirit should encourage both Catholics and Orthodox, especially in the cultural, spiritual, pastoral, educational and social fields, avoiding any temptation to undue zeal for their own community to the disadvantage of the other. May the good of Christ's Church always prevail! Mutual support and the exchange of gifts can only make pastoral activity itself more effective and our witness to the Gospel we desire to proclaim more transparent."

5. "We maintain that a more active and concerted collaboration will also facilitate the Church's influence in promoting peace and justice in situations of political or ethnic conflict. The Christian faith has unprecedented possibilities for solving humanity's tensions and enmity."

Evangelicals and Catholics Together
The Christian Mission in the Third Millennium: Conclusion

"We do know that his promise is sure, that we are enlisted for the duration, and that we are in this together. We do know that we must affirm and hope and search and contend and witness together, for we belong not to ourselves but to him who purchased us by the blood of the cross. We do know that this is a time of opportunity—and, if of opportunity, then of responsibility—for Evangelicals and Catholics to be Christians together in a way that helps prepare the world for the coming of him to whom belongs the kingdom, the power and the glory forever. Amen."

Ecumenism and the Nature of Church

In the Sword of the Spirit, we believe in the need for ecumenical cooperation in support of the gospel and as an expression of the intrinsic unity that is the work of the Holy Spirit. We believe this word of ecumenical cooperation is a part of the modern Pentecost that we see sweeping the globe. We are privileged to be a part of this grass-roots ecumenical movement that has emerged in the last few decades after hundreds of years of Christian division.

Some of our communities are ecumenical in membership and by design. Some of our communities are denominational in membership and by design. All of our communities are ecumenical in ethos, and our regional and international events can be quite a blend of denominational expressions from around the world.

We believe that the ecumenical reality is an element of the nature of the modern Christian church and that ecumenical cooperation is being restored by the Holy Spirit in our time.

COVENANT CHRISTIAN COMMUNITY

In the Sword of the Spirit we say that we are in covenant together, at the local level, and at the international level. Our covenants are unique at the local level, but they all contain a paragraph that describes our relationship to the international community of communities. The issue could be easily raised as to whether or not a written covenant is necessary, or whether or not it can be described as a part of the nature of life in the Body of Christ. We believe that the Lord has called us into covenant with him and with this people. We have had numerous prophecies that have initiated and sustained that understanding. Here are some excerpts:

"I am making a covenant with you…this covenant is part of my plan to renew my church…"

"Yes, I have called you together in a covenant that is of great significance for the life of my people throughout the world, and I want you to bind yourselves to me and show forth your loyalty to me. I want you to come to me under this covenant, submit yourselves to my service, lay down your lives for the mission that I have given you."

Exodus 19:5 says, "Now therefore, obey my voice and keep my covenant and be my possession." It could be said here that the prophecies are for us, for those to whom they were spoken. It could also be said that the scripture given is for the Old Testament folks, or more narrowly, for those that the prophet addressed. We would not say that all Christians or Christian groups should sit down and write a covenant, but we do think we have something to contribute in this area. Furthermore, since the Bible is broken into the Old and New Testaments (covenants), it may be the case that the Lord does have certain expectations on his New Testament people based on his covenant with us, sealed by the blood of his son.

We have been led in our local communities to attempt to identify and summarize that greater covenant and to commit ourselves together in covenant relationships.

The Roman Catholic Bishop James A. Griffin talked about commitment this way:

> "Words like commitment, compassion and empathy have no place in the world of objects," said Bishop Griffin.
> Individual relationships in our society are characterized by looser connections. We're no longer joiners living out commitments in fraternal or social groups. We've become more individualistic. Individual fulfillment is more important. ...If this is where we find ourselves, is there any antidote for the loose connections? The solution is found in commitment.
> "We learn this in the family, which is the root of all relationships. Within every family there is a commitment to all the members of the family and a shared commitment to a common value system," he added.
> "Without commitment, there can be no lasting relationships", said Bishop Griffin, and "barriers are insurmountable. Disagreements are destructive. Shortcomings are terminal. Commitment allows individuals' lack to be filled up with gifts of others."[1]

More Covenant Background

Pertinent Questions

What are the needs in society today? How is the Lord addressing those needs? What is there about our call that is unique, or important or prophetic? Society today is increasingly unstable, increasingly disconnected. We see a profound example of this at the family level where many marriages have failed and many families have unraveled at the altars of individualistic hedonism and narcissism. The Lord wants a people where unity is a blessing, and to be scattered is seen as a curse. It is not good when members of a family run in every direction, each pursuing his own path to self-fulfillment. If we consider the marriage covenant and the divorce rate, we can identify and target one of the major threats to the stability and strength of the family, to society, and to the church. If making and keeping covenants strengthens and supports marriages, we would have ample reason for seeing value in our life together. It is the case that covenant communities have divorce rates far below that of most churches. That result is important and prophetic. The Lord is addressing a need.

Types of Covenants

There are many types of covenants: solemn, implied, simple, legal, simple-legal, limited duration, etc. An example of an implied contract is when a paper boy delivers a paper for weeks and is paid weekly. There is then an *implied* covenant that if he delivers the paper next week, he will get one week's pay. It is also implied that his price will be the same.

I'd like to describe marriage as an *expansive* covenant: The vows may have been simple and limited, but there is a much broader understanding of what a man and woman are entering into as husband, as wife, as father, and as mother. There are legal, spiritual, and societal expectations that go beyond, "I will be a friend to you." So too with us; when we agree to follow the Lord together, to be faithful to him and to each other, it is broader than the few elements that we identify in our local covenants. But, we would certainly like to focus on and get those elements to work. We would get a long way into the Christian life if we took our covenants seriously.

The Covenant Nature of God

Trinity

We see first in the Trinity a clearly defined relationship of a certain order, of fierce loyalty, of covenant love. Jesus knew his role and his relationship to the Father and to the Holy Spirit; the Father spoke of his Son, and the Spirit gives testimony to Jesus in the hearts of millions daily. Is there a written covenant among the Father, Son and Spirit? I don't know. But their relationship is clear, and clearly defined.

God and Man

All through the Bible we see the Lord entering into agreements with man, promising certain things in return for certain obedience. These agreements and promises have theological names based on persons and places (Davidic, Edenic, Sinaitic, Abrahamic, etc.), but each one shows certain aspects of the covenant nature of God: 1) his faithfulness (he will do his part); 2) his justice (he requires our part); 3) his tenacity (he is determined to get mankind on the right track and into his family); 4) his desire to "deal" with man. There is also a progressive nature to these covenants as mankind is shepherded more closely onto the path that leads back to God. We see the culmination of God's covenant nature with the life, death and resurrection of Jesus Christ. He will go to great lengths to keep his side of the deal: *the sacrifice of his son.*

There is an algebraic rule which states that if "A=B" and "B=C", then "A=B=C." In a certain way we are acting in a similar fashion. That is, if the Trinity has a clearly defined relationship and God defines his relationship with man, then it is good for brothers and sisters to have clearly defined relationships. We attempt to mimic our Father, to relate the way he relates, and to take on the covenant nature of God.

Covenant in Scripture

Berith

The word "covenant" is used as a translation for the Hebrew word "berith" in the Old Testament. That word literally means "fetter" or "bind," but it also means "to eat with." For the Hebrews, it was a serious thing to have a meal with someone. In the New Testament, the Lord's Supper is the covenant meal of the Christian. It is where and how we celebrate our "deal" with the Lord…the deal that gets us into heaven and delivers us from the fires of hell. The words translated "covenant" show up about ninety times in the Old Testament and twenty-eight times in the New Testament. It is clearly a major theme, an important way of describing the character and intentions of God.

Three Types
There are three types of covenants common in scripture:
1) A two-sided agreement between equals (David and Jonathan; see example next section);
2) A one-sided disposition imposed by a superior party; and
3) God's self-imposed obligation (our redemption by the work of Christ is in this category).

Serious Intentions Require Serious Tools

Difficult Assignments
Close brotherhood and Christian mission are often complex endeavors. We saw in the New Testament that John Mark did not complete his mission as Paul expected and was subsequently excluded from the next mission (Acts 15:38). Marriage is a complex journey which is begun (and not until) with marriage vows. We have "confessing" churches, and "rules" for religious orders. These defined relationships have taken an approach that puts them at odds with our shifting-sands culture. Our shifting-sands culture affects both marriage and mission.

At Stake
At stake are survival, continuity, endurance, longevity and trans-generational strength. Our word should be important; our covenants are a blueprint for the present as well as a seed for future generations. They are a mix of God and man, and express our best efforts to describe our intended response to him and to each other.

Summary
1) Covenants are serious.
2) Covenants are serious tools for serious intentions (community, discipleship, mission, all require covenant).
3) Covenants are serious because our WORD should be serious.
4) Covenant-breaking unravels relationships: the family, society and the Church.
5) Covenant reflects the very nature of God.
6) Covenant reflects the relationship of the Trinity.

7) Restoring covenant is one of the key works of God being introduced to us and then shown through us (a gift from the Lord to meet a need).
8) It is not the idea or the invention of some prophets of a movement.
9) It is ancient, widely expressed in scripture, and in Church life, in civil law, and in marriage.
10) The inability to commit, the inability to honor and to keep your word is a modern fatal flaw…a need that is being addressed by God.
11) Covenant is trans-generational, but must be fully embraced in nature and fully embraced with character to benefit from its blessing.

A Scriptural Example

In a quick study of Ruth, we see it begins with the widow Naomi instructing her Moabite daughters-in-law to return to their own land now that her two sons have died. Ruth says, "Wherever you go I shall go, wherever you live I shall live; your people will be my people, and your God will be my God too" (Ruth 1:16 paraphrased). This example of covenant love works out well for Ruth who marries Boaz. They have a son, Obed, who was the father of Jesse, the father of David.

So covenant love and faithfulness is in the line of David. The very next book in the Old Testament is 1 Samuel. In 1 Samuel, we see the story of Samuel, the story of Saul and the story of David (1 Samuel 16).

Covenant Lived Out

The knitting of the souls of Jonathan and David; Jonathan and David make a covenant (1 Samuel 18:1-5)
"When he had finished speaking to Saul, the soul of Jonathan was knit to the soul of David, and Jonathan loved him as his own soul. And Saul took him that day and would not let him return to his own house. Then Jonathan made a covenant with David, because he loved him as his own soul. And Jonathan stripped himself of the robe that was upon him, and gave it to David, and his armor, and even his sword and his bow and his girdle. And David went out and was successful wherever Saul sent him; so that Saul set him over the men of war. And this was good in the sight of all the people and also in the sight of Saul's servants."

The outbreak of jealousy in the heart of Saul (1 Samuel 18:6-9) *"As they were coming home, when David returned from slaying the Philistine, the women came out of all the cities of Israel, singing and dancing, to meet King Saul, with timbrels, with songs of joy, and with instruments of music. And the women sang to one another as they made merry, "Saul has slain his thousands, and David his ten thousands." And Saul was very angry, and this saying displeased him; he said, "They have ascribed to David ten thousands and to me they have ascribed thousands; and what more can he have but the kingdom?" And Saul eyed David from that day on."*

The attempted murder of David by the now insane Saul (1 Samuel 18:10-12) *"And on the morrow an evil spirit from God rushed upon Saul, and he raved within his house, while David was playing the lyre, as he did day by day. Saul had his spear in his hand; and Saul cast the spear, for he thought, "I will pin David to the wall." But David evaded him twice."*

Things continue to deteriorate between Saul and David, yet the covenant stands (1 Samuel 20:3-4; 8a) *"But David replied, 'Your father knows well that I have found favor in your eyes; and he thinks, 'Let not Jonathan know this, lest he be grieved.' But truly, as the Lord lives, and as your soul lives, there is but a step between me and death.' Then said Jonathan to David, "Whatever you say, I will do for you…(David replied,) "Therefore deal kindly with your servant, for you have brought your servant into a sacred covenant with you."*

The covenant extends to family (1 Samuel 20:14-17) *"'If I am still alive, show me the loyal love of the Lord, that I may not die; and do not cut off your loyalty from my house for ever. When the Lord cuts off every one of the enemies of David from the face of the earth, let not the name of Jonathan be cut off from the house of David. And may the Lord take vengeance on David's enemies.' And Jonathan then made David swear again by his love for him; for he loved him as he loved his own soul."*

The covenant is reiterated (1 Samuel 20:23) *"And as for the matter of which you and I have spoken, behold, the Lord is between you and me forever."*

The covenant is reiterated as trans-generational (1 Samuel 20:41-42) *"And as soon as the lad had gone, David rose from beside the stone heap and fell on his face to the ground, and bowed three times; and they kissed one another and wept with one another, until David recovered himself. Then Jonathan said to David, "Go in peace, forasmuch as we have sworn both of us in the name of the Lord, saying, "The Lord shall be between me and you, and between my descendants and your descendants, forever."*

BOB TEDESCO

Recommitment night (1 Samuel 23:15-18) *"And David was afraid because Saul had come out to seek his life. David was in the wilderness of Ziph at Horesh. And Jonathan, Saul's son, rose, and went to David at Horesh, and strengthened his hand in God. And he said to him, "Fear not; for the hand of Saul my father shall not find you; you shall be king over Israel, and I shall be next to you; Saul my father also knows this." And the two of them made a covenant before the Lord."*

Saul and David remain at odds (2 Samuel 3:1) *"There was a long war between the house of Saul and the house of David; and David grew stronger and stronger, while the house of Saul became weaker and weaker."*

Saul and Jonathan die (1 Samuel 31:2, 4c) *"And the Philistines overtook Saul and his sons; and the Philistines slew Jonathan and Abinadab and Mal'chishu'a, the sons of Saul...Therefore Saul took his own sword and fell upon it."*

The introduction of Jonathan's son (2 Samuel 4:4) *"Jonathan, the son of Saul, had a son who was crippled in his feet, Mephib'osheth."*

The covenant extends to Jonathan's family (2 Samuel 9: 1-13) *And David said, "Is there still any one left of the house of Saul, that I may show him kindness for Jonathan's sake?" Ziba replied, 'There is still a son of Jonathan; he is crippled in his feet." The king said to him, "Where is he?" And Ziba said to the king, "He is in the house of Machir the son of Am'miel, at Lo'debar. Then King David sent and brought him from the house of Machir the son of Am'miel, at Lo'debar. And Mephib'osheth, the son of Jonathan, the son of Saul, came to David, and fell on his face and did obeisance. And David said, "Mephib'osheth!" And he answered, "Behold, your servant." And David said to him, "Fear not for I will show kindness for the sake of your father Jonathan, and I will restore to you all the land of Saul your father; and you shall eat at my table always." And he did obeisance, and said, "What is your servant, that you should look upon a dead dog such as I?"*

Then the king called Ziba, Saul's servant, and said to him, "All that belonged to Saul and to all his house I have given to your master's son. And you and your sons and your servants shall till the land for him, and shall bring in the produce, that your master's son may have bread to eat; but Mephib'osheth your master's son shall always eat at my table." Now Ziba had fifteen sons and twenty servants. Then Ziba said to the king, "According to all that my lord the king commands his servant, so will your servant do." So Mephib'osheth ate at David's table, like one of the king's sons. And Mephib'osheth had a young son whose name was Mica. And all who dwelt in Ziba's house became

Mephib'osheth's servants. So Mephib'osheth dwelt in Jerusalem; for he ate always at the king's table. Now he was lame in both his feet.

Note: In ancient times a covenant in blood was not uncommon. Each man would make a small cut at the base of his thumb and the two would bring their two hands together and mix the blood as a sign of being joined together. Some think that this covenant of David and Jonathan was a "blood covenant."

TAKING A TRANS-GENERATIONAL APPROACH

In the Sword of the Spirit, we have, for many years now, taken a trans-generational approach to community life, structures and programs. That is to say, we believe that our children share in the vision and the call that we have been given; we believe we have been called *as families* into Christian community. We know that some might receive a different call from the Lord, and also that some may freely choose not to respond, but we are taking an approach that attempts to pass on our vision, our call, and our faith to our children. We want them to benefit from the gift that the Lord has given to us.

Scripture is Trans-generational

Blessings

Blessings (vision, call, faith, prosperity) are often cited as extending out to future generations.

> *"I will indeed bless you, and I will multiply your descendants as the stars of heaven and as the sand which is on the seashore. And your descendants shall possess the gate of their enemies, and by your descendants shall all the nations of the earth bless themselves, because you have obeyed my voice."* Genesis 22:17-18

"God Almighty bless you and make you fruitful and multiply you that you might become a company of peoples. May He give the blessing of Abraham to you and to your descendants with you, that you may take possession of the land of your sojournings which God gave to Abraham!" Genesis 28:3-4

"Make haste and go up to my father and say to him, 'Thus says your son Joseph, God has made me lord of all Egypt; come down to me, do not tarry; you shall dwell in the land of Goshen, and you shall be near me, you and your children and your children's children, and your flocks, your herds, and all that you have; and there I will provide for you, for there are yet five years of famine to come; lest you and your household, and all that you have, come to poverty.'" Genesis 45:9-11

Curses and Punishments

Curses and punishments are likewise not limited to only those who have earned them. (Life, it seems, is not "fair" by our standards.)

"And I tell him that I am about to punish his house forever, for the iniquity that he knew, because his sons were blaspheming God, and he did not restrain them. Therefore I swear to the house of Eli that the iniquity of Eli's house shall not be expiated by sacrifice or offering for ever." 1 Samuel 3:13-14

"David said to Nathan, "I have sinned against the Lord." And Nathan said to David, "The Lord also has put away your sin; you shall not die. Nevertheless, because by this deed you have utterly scorned the Lord, the child that is born to you shall die." 2 Samuel 12:13-14

Covenant

Covenant is trans-generational:

"And the two of them made a covenant before the Lord; David remained at Horesh, and Jonathan went home." 1 Samuel 23:18

"And Mephibosheth, the son of Jonathan, the son of Saul, came to David, and fell on his face and did obeisance. And David said, "Mephibosheth!" And he answered, "Behold, your servant." And David said to him, "Do not fear, for I will show you kindness for the sake of your father Jonathan, and I will restore to you all the land of Saul your father; and you shall eat at my table always." 2 Samuel 9:6-7

This trans-generational pattern is not just in the Old Testament:

> "And they said, "Believe in the Lord Jesus and you will be saved, <u>you and your household</u>." And they spoke the word of the Lord to him and to all that were in his house. And he took them the same hour of the night, and washed their wounds, and he was baptized at once, with all his family." Acts 16:31-33

Obedience/blessing

> "Honor your father and mother (this is the first commandment with a promise) that it may be well with you and you may live long on the earth." Ephesians 6:2-3

The New Testament also takes a concern for young and old "in the Lord" and "faith generations" are addressed.

> "To Timothy, my true child in the faith: Grace, mercy, and peace from God the Father and Christ Jesus our Lord." 1 Timothy 1:2

> "You then, my son, be strong in the grace that is in Christ Jesus..." 2 Timothy 2:1

> "But we were gentle among you, like a nurse taking care of her children." 1 Thessalonians 2:7

> "...for you know how, like a father with his children, we exhorted each one of you and encouraged you and charged you..." 1 Thessalonians 2:11

> "I am reminded of your sincere faith, a faith that dwelt first in your grandmother Lois and your mother Eunice and now, I am sure, dwells in you." 2 Timothy 1:5

<u>Four generations</u> of Christian faith are shown in 2 Timothy 2:2. "...And what you have heard from me before many witnesses entrust to faithful men who will be able to teach others also."

What you have received

Even certain godly practices, such as tithing, are shown as trans-generational.

"One might say that even Levi himself, who receives tithes, paid tithes through Abraham, for he was still in the loins of Abraham when Melchizedek met him." Hebrews 7:9-10

Training and influence

The Bible never presupposes that children will just grow up and make their choices in a vacuum, but that they will be trained and influenced by the parents…and grandparents.

"You shall therefore lay up these words of mine in your heart and in your soul; and you shall bind them as a sign on you hand, and they shall be as frontlets between your eyes. And you shall teach them to your children, talking of them when you are sitting in your house, and when you are walking by the way, and when you lie down, and when you rise. And you shall write them upon the doorposts of your house and upon your gates, that your days and the days of your children may be multiplied in the land which the Lord swore to your fathers to give them, as long as the heavens are above the earth." Deuteronomy 11:18-21

Mother, grandmother

"I am reminded of your sincere faith, a faith that dwelt first in your grandmother Lois, and your mother Eunice and now, I am sure, dwells in you." 1 Timothy 1:5

Go…make…teach…:

"Go therefore and make disciples of all nations, baptizing them in the name of the Father and of the Son and of the Holy Spirit, teaching them to observe all that I have commanded you…" Matthew 28:19-20a

Raise them up (elevate to):

Fathers, do not provoke your children to anger, but bring them up in the discipline and instruction of the Lord. Ephesians 6:4

Accepting the Call

A Conversion

For many parents, something like a conversion is needed. Whether we are in a Christian community or not, passing on faith to the next generation is a lot of work. Accepting the Lord personally presents a challenge to our desires, our habits, and our patterns of life. To pass on the faith to the next generation will demand more of us and even deeper values and patterns will be rattled, disturbed, and shaken.

First Step

The first step to a trans-generational community is for parents and single people to agree that this is the Lord's will. A certain process led us to conclude that the Lord has called us, and that means more than just a singular response. It was a call to become part of his people as *disciples*, entering a process of formation and embracing a mission. More than an altar call is needed for our children as well. For some individuals and communities, a retreat weekend might be helpful in coming to a conviction and a commitment to this course.

Trans-generational Approaches

As a Family

Some of the main influences in how we live our family life are our hopes and dreams for our children. If our hopes are mainly for academic excellence, that will direct a certain approach. If we are mainly focused on athletic accomplishments, a different approach is needed. If we want children to be active and fully engaged in the school culture, something very different is needed. I have known some parents who just wanted their children to grow up and go away… (but be "saved"). Less is needed with this approach. If we want our children to be disciples of Jesus Christ, formed into his kingdom and mainly living for him, a new approach is needed. *We will be teaching them to see things through his eyes not their own.* We will be teaching them to make personal decisions based on what is best for his people and not for the self. Self-image, self-fulfillment, self-help, etc. has become the mantra of the modern culture. I am surprised that we are not yet finding students chanting, "self, self, self…" in the high school classrooms. A trans-generational approach to family/community life will bring decisions about career, academics, sports, recreation, activities, and friendships under the influence of, "What is best for the kingdom of God?"

As a Community

Trans-generational community life will make major demands

on the structures and the leadership of a Christian community. Programs, activities, events, retreats, gatherings, etc. will now have to take a growing concern for passing on the vision and life to the next generations. Leadership and ministry teams will have to work at drawing in younger folks. Time, money and prayer will have to be directed to things like summer camp, high school programs, campus outreaches, and post-college initiation groups. A smooth, coherent plan should be developed which allows a child to grow, encounter the Lord, develop as a disciple, and take a place alongside other mature Christians. In the Sword of the Spirit we are fortunate to have regional youth programs with retreats, mission trips, periods of service, and training beyond the local community. If a local community is too small to do much, at least the regional programs and connections are there to help.

Obstacles

Time Bombs and Land Mines

Life sometimes is marred by things that blow up in our faces. The "land mine" metaphor describes those things that are unexpected or seemingly impossible to predict: a serious illness, a car accident, a house fire. The "time bombs" of life are a bit different: we can almost see them coming. They may not be unexpected, but their impact can be worse than we thought: retirement, the failure of a business, the failure of a relationship.

For those raising children, the examples can be quite different. Land mines might be our son's loss of interest in school with his new awareness of girls, our daughter's decision to forego college for a naval career, or our daughter's choice of a college hundreds of miles from family and community. Time bombs might be things like the impact of elementary school on a child, the onset of puberty, or college tuition expenses.

I am of the view that many of life's unexpected explosions are actually more predictable and less surprising to those with more experience, who know the end results of certain patterns of life and decision making.

Big Obstacles (See Appendix D)

We have learned over the years that certain obstacles have a profound impact on our trans-generational vision. An early one might be our choice of school. When parents pick a school or school system, they are also unwittingly choosing a set of friends for their child. Recreational dating* is another big obstacle along with an approach to courtship that is not "faith-based" or consistent with our perceived call from the Lord.

Correspondingly, the choice of spouse that does not support our life's call is usually devastating. The choice of college or school can be another obstacle along with the choice of career. To pursue a career as a helicopter pilot in the U.S. Army is unlikely to also result in being in a Christian community. (Although I do know one who made the transition!) These are all decisions that set a course for our children and to the degree that they are disconnecting them from the body of Christ, they are damaging (often fatal) to a trans-generational vision.

A Descriptive Equation

We can look at this trans-generational call as a spiritual equation. On one side, we have the next generation making decisions to enter our communities. On the other side of the equal sign are the factors contributing to or detracting them from making that choice: the parents, the children, the family, the Lord, the enemy, the world, and the community. These are not all of the factors and we won't discuss all of these. Nor will we discuss any of these in the depth needed.** Stated another way, "How do the parents, the children, and the community affect the number of children coming into the community".

Parents

As parents, our underlying attitudes toward the Lord, his kingdom, and his people will greatly affect our ability to inspire respect and admiration from our children for our way of life. Sometimes we want something at one level that is not supported by the way we talk or act. (Perhaps we tend to be sarcastic, critical, or negative). Our children are adept at sensing those contradictions. They are keenly aware if we are mainly impressed by academic excellence or worldly success. Are Christian leaders or pioneers, our heroes? Or is it Donald Trump, or Bill Gates, or the latest Nobel Prize winner?

In addition to supportive attitudes and speech, I would point to *parents having a plan* (and a budget) for getting each child fully engaged in the kingdom life that the Lord has given to us. This will often involve choices as well as the painful decisions to forego certain "opportunities" for our children's development. "*Immediately* they left their nets and followed him." Mt 4:21-22

Family

The family environment should be one that supports transgenerational community life. Our daily life patterns (meals, prayer, free time), our weekly life pattern (our gatherings for worship, celebrating the Lord's Day, etc.) and our special events (retreats, conferences, vacations), should all be ordered in a way that is supportive of our calling.

Additionally, the ways that we honor each other on a daily basis and at special events can have a huge impact over a period of time. Each family should look for ways to establish daily, weekly, and special event approaches to honoring. We can talk it through together and then we can do it. There is a toxic, sarcastic negativity to much modern speech and commentary. Honoring each other is one antidote to that poison.

Children

Children need to honor their parents and obey them. They need to be able to see that this will be the main way (early on) that they love the Lord. Obedience to parents is one expression of loving God. We should tell them this truth. Children need to know and experience that the Lord is at the center of this family and that this family's joy is in loving and serving God and accepting his order. As children, we can *enjoy* youth group, Lord's Day celebrations, retreat, campouts, etc.

The Community

The first and main step for a community is to have a plan inspired by the Lord: a plan with a vision, a plan that includes educating and supporting both the parents and the children in its vision. When a community knows where it is going, it can then develop action steps that involve approaches, resources, and personnel. It can also tap into regional or outside resources and programs that support its vision.

The World, the Flesh, and the Devil

Many obstacles will present themselves along the way, and children who have been raised in good, clear-thinking and clear-sighted families will have the best chances of surviving the gauntlet. Having said that, we should remember that the heaviest positive element of this equation is the grace and the mercy of God! Some children who have come from family situations that were confused or chaotic have still done well in the kingdom of God. The Lord can overcome all of our weaknesses, obstacles, and confusions as families.

Summary

1) Have a plan (regional, community, family).
2) Commit yourselves to it (mind, heart, patterns of speech, patterns of life, time and money).
3) Beseech the Lord constantly, expecting miracles!

*Dating with no purpose or intention of marriage either possible or expected.
**This subject is part of a later intended work.

FREEDOM AND LIFE'S PLANS

- *We are free to live our lives however we desire...* or so the story goes.
- *We are free to follow our dreams and desires, as long as we do not hurt anyone...* or so the story goes on.
- *We are free to follow our dreams and desires, as long as we do not disobey God...* or so the story goes on and on...

In this chapter we will explore a bit the purposes of our lives. We will consider the range of approaches from sin (negative) to a benign pursuit of personal desires (neutral) to bearing some fruit (positive), to finding God's will for our lives (Plan A). We will mainly rely on scriptural examples, even though life's examples and other Christian teaching could be employed.

Negative - Sin

Clearly, a sinful approach to life has deadly consequences.

> *"And another portent appeared in heaven; behold, a great red dragon, with seven heads and ten horns, and seven diadems upon his heads. His tail swept down a third of the stars of heaven, and cast them to the earth. And the dragon stood before the woman who was about to bear a child, that he might devour her child when she brought it forth;..."Revelation 12:3-4*

> "Now war arose in heaven, Michael and his angels fighting against the dragon; and the dragon and his angels fought, but they were defeated and there was no longer any place for them in heaven. And the great dragon was thrown down, that ancient serpent, who is called the Devil and Satan, the deceiver of the whole world—he was thrown down to the earth, and his angels were thrown down with him." Revelation 12:7-9

Lucifer and his angels were not allowed to stay in heaven. (Revelation 12:8)

> "But Peter said, 'Ananias, why has Satan filled your heart to lie to the Holy Spirit and to keep part of the proceeds of the land? While it remained unsold, did it not remain your own? And after it was sold, was it not at your disposal? How is it that you have contrived this deed in your heart? You have not lied to men but to God.' When Ananias heard these words, he fell down and died. And great fear came upon all who heard of it. The young men rose and wrapped him up and carried him out and buried him." Acts 5:3-6

> "Do you not know that the unrighteous will not inherit the kingdom of God? Do not be deceived; neither the immoral, nor idolaters, nor sexual perverts, nor thieves, nor the greedy, nor drunkards, nor revilers, nor robbers will inherit the kingdom of God. And such were some of you. But you were washed, you were sanctified, you were justified in the name of the Lord Jesus Christ and in the Spirit of our God."
> 1 Corinthians 6:9-10
> "'All things are lawful for me,' but not all things are helpful. 'All things are lawful for me, but I will not be enslaved by anything." 1 Corinthians 6:12

Neutral

Pursuing my dreams and desires (even without apparently breaking any rules, our natural tendencies, desires and dreams may not lead us in the best direction)

> "Whatever a man sows, that he will also reap. For he who sows to his own flesh, reaps corruption; but he who sows to the Spirit will from the Spirit reap eternal life." Galatians 6:7b-8

> "For you were called to freedom, brethren; only do not use your freedom as an opportunity for the flesh, but through love be servants of one another." Galatians 5:13

"Because you are lukewarm, and neither cold nor hot, I will spew you out of my mouth." Revelation 3:16

"For whoever would save his life will lose it; and whoever loses his life for my sake, he will save it. For what does it profit a man if he gains the whole world and loses or forfeits himself? For whoever is ashamed of me and of my words, of him will the Son of man be ashamed when he comes in his glory and the glory of the Father and of the holy angels." Luke 9:24-26

"In the morning, as he was returning to the city, he was hungry. And seeing a fig tree by the wayside he went to it, and found nothing on it but leaves only. And he said to it, "May no fruit ever come from you again!" And the fig tree withered at once." Matthew. 21:18-19

"Hear then the parable of the sower. When anyone hears the word of the kingdom and does not understand it, the evil one comes and snatches away what is sown in his heart; this is what was sown along the path. As for what was sown on the rocky ground, this is he who hears the word and immediately receives it with joy; yet he has no root in himself, but endures for a while, and when tribulation or persecution arises on account of the word, immediately he falls away. As for what was sown among thorns, this is he who hears the word, but the cares of the world and the delight in riches choke the word, and it proves unfruitful. As for what was sown on good soil, this is he who hears the word and understands it; he indeed bears fruit, and yields, in one case a hundredfold, in another sixty, and in another thirty." Matthew 13:18-23

Positive

Bearing Some Fruit: the gamble of a measured response

"And behold, one came up to him, saying, 'Teacher, what good deed must I do, to have eternal life?' And he said to him, 'Why do you ask me about what is good? One there is who is good. If you would enter life, keep the commandments.' He said to him, 'Which?' And Jesus said, 'You shall not kill, You shall not commit adultery, You shall not steal, You shall not bear false witness, Honor your father and mother, and, You shall love your neighbor as yourself.' The young man said to him, 'All these I have observed; what do I still lack?' Jesus said to him, 'If you would be perfect, go, sell what you possess and give to the poor, and you will have treasure in heaven; and come, follow me.' When the young man heard this, he went away sorrowful; for he had great possessions. And Jesus said to his disciples, 'Truly, I say to you, it will be hard for a rich man to enter the kingdom of heaven. Again I tell you, it is easier for a camel to go through the eye of a needle than for a rich man to enter the kingdom of God.'" Matthew 19:16-24

What "success" do we hope for our children?

> *"If you love those who love you, what credit is that to you? For even sinners love those who love them. And if you do good to those who do good to you, what credit is that to you? For even sinners do the same."* Luke 6:32-33
> *"Take heed then how you hear; for to him who has will more be given, and from him who has not, even what he thinks that he has will be taken away."* Luke 8:18

> *"To the angel of the church in Ephesus write: 'The words of him who holds the seven stars in his right hand, who walks among the seven golden lamp stands. I know your works, your toil and your patient endurance, and how you cannot bear evil men but have tested those who call themselves apostles but are not, and found them to be false; I know you are enduring patiently and bearing up for my name's sake, and you have not grown weary. But I have this against you: that you have abandoned the love you had at first. Remember then from what you have fallen, repent and do the works you did at first. If not, I will come to you and remove your lamp stand from its place, unless you repent.'"* Revelation 2:1-5

As we can see in the previous verses from Revelation, the church at Ephesus had borne some fruit, but was now in some trouble.

> *"When he returned, having received the kingdom, he commanded these servants, to whom he had given the money, to be called to him, that he might know what they had gained by trading. The first came before him, saying, 'Lord, your pound has made ten pounds more.' And he said to him, 'Well done good servant! Because you have been faithful in a very little, you shall have authority over ten cities.' And the second came, saying, 'Lord, your pound has made five pounds.' And he said to him, 'And you are to be over five cities.' Then another came, saying, 'Lord, here is your pound, which I kept laid away in a napkin; for I was afraid of you, because you are a severe man; you take up what you did not lay down, and reap what you did not sow.' He said to him, 'I will condemn you out of your own mouth, you wicked servant!' You knew that I was a severe man, taking up what I did not lay down and reaping what I did not sow? Why then did you not put my money into the bank, and at my coming I should have collected it with interest?'"* Luke 19:15-23

You could conclude from this story that the king is happy with any amount of return. Another way to look at it: both of those who brought a return had to risk what they were given, and they did. One was more successful, but both took the necessary risk. Neither selfishly held back. Notice also that verse 23 addresses the earlier "neutral" approach.

Plan A - Going all out, inspired life

But I say, walk by the Spirit and do not gratify the desires of the flesh. Galatians 5:16

If we live by the Spirit, let us also walk by the Spirit. Let us have no self-conceit, no provoking of one another, no envy of one another. Galatians 5:25-26

"The body is not meant for immorality, but for the Lord, and the Lord for the body." 1 Corinthians 6:13c
"But he who is united to the Lord becomes one spirit with him." 1 Corinthians 6:17

"You are not your own; you were bought with a price. So glorify God in your body." 1 Corinthians 6:19c-20

"…but through love be servants of one another. For the whole law is fulfilled in one word, 'You shall love your neighbor as yourself.'" Galatians 5:13c-14

"Therefore, I tell you, the kingdom of God will be taken away from you and given to a nation producing the fruits of it." Matthew 21: 43

"Again, the kingdom of God is like a merchant in search of fine pearls, who, on finding one pearl of great value, went and sold all that he had and bought it." Matthew 13:45-46

So, it would seem that *there is a "Plan A" for our lives,* and we are intended to bear *much* fruit for the kingdom. Some of our plans and career paths may be a part of that plan, but we are not just called to self-fulfillment, good self-image, and the enjoyment of life and creation. Paul mentioned these options when he wrote to the Corinthians.

"For if I preach the gospel, that gives me no ground for boasting. For necessity is laid upon me. Woe to me if I do not preach the gospel! For if I do this of my own will, I have a reward; but if not of my own will, I am entrusted with a commission." 1 Corinthians 9:16-17

"For though I am free from all men, I have made myself a slave to all, that I might win the more." 1 Corinthians 9:19

"I do it all for the sake of the gospel that I may share in its blessings. Do you not know that in a race all the runners compete, but only one receives the prize? So run that you may obtain it. Every athlete exercises self-control in all things. They do it to receive a perishable wreath, but we an imperishable. Well, I do not run aimlessly, I do not box as one beating the air; but I pommel my body and subdue it, lest after preaching to others I myself should be disqualified." 1 Corinthians 9:23-27

Our lives should bear fruit for the kingdom; we should raise our children to expect to bear fruit for the kingdom. (If single, or if we do not have children, we should support those raising children to be disciples). We should train them to see with the eyes of the kingdom and not with the eyes of the self; we should train them to hear with the ears of the kingdom and not with the ears of the self. We should raise them to know that it (fruit) will come at a cost; we should raise them to know that the reward will far surpass the cost.

"Then Peter said in reply, "Lo, we have left everything and followed you. What then shall we have?" Jesus said to them, "Truly, I say to you, in the new world, when the Son of man shall sit on his glorious throne, you who have followed me will also sit on twelve thrones, judging the twelve tribes of Israel. And every one who has left houses or brothers or sisters or father or mother or children or lands, for my name's sake, will receive a hundredfold, and inherit eternal life." Matthew 19:27-29

A COMMUNITY OF DISCIPLES ON MISSION

In the Sword of the Spirit, we say that we are a "community of disciples on mission." Much has already been written about this phrase, and I hope only to give an additional perspective. I believe that this is one of those areas where all Christian churches could benefit from a re-examination of each element, and, hopefully, this might result in a deeper commitment to each characteristic of the Christian life.

"A Community"

Uses

As mentioned earlier, "community" is a word that can have many meanings and many applications. I was surprised to read a Model Airplane News editorial which spoke about the "modeling community", and even spoke of "brothers and sisters" in modeling! So, some applications of the word can be functional or activity-oriented: the banking community, the racing community, prayer community, etc. These functions can and do involve relationships, but it is often the function that initiates and holds the relationship together.

Other uses of the word have a more relational intent, while some groupings *imply* community without using the word: family and convent. In these cases certain activities are implied, but the relationship continues by definition, whether or not certain activities continue. I was a member of my parents' family long after I was not there for evening meals. Members of a religious order can change the focus of their work while maintaining their relationship and way of life.

A brief description

Covenant Christian community is first of all *Christian* followers of Christ. It is a set of intentional relationships (not necessarily family) where the members seek to live a common way of life described by their covenant. This relational aspect of community must be carefully fostered and nurtured to keep from drifting into becoming functional in our expression of community life. If we overly identify with our activities, we can lose the "brother – sister" aspect intended for the family of God. We might not care for the lonely, strengthen the weak, visit the sick or comfort the mourning. We are brothers and sisters for eternity, and I need to care about your life in the "here and now".

Within the Sword of the Spirit there are varieties of expressions that result in brothers and sisters spending more or less time together; yet we pursue a common way of life. A single person living with a community family will spend more time with community members than if living alone. Folks living in a cluster (community neighborhood) will find it easier to be together or see one another than those living at a distance from each other. Time together is an essential aspect of relational strength, and decisions should be approached with the question, *"Will this decision mean more community or less community?"* If we decide that our son should be an Olympic ice skater, we might never see the Body of Christ again! Moving to that great house 25 miles away may not be as wise as the less-than-perfect house in a community cluster.

So, community is intentional; it is relational; it involves spending time together; and it should be a factor to consider in significant life decisions.

"Of Disciples"

Believers

I would like to make a risky distinction here between believers and disciples. It's risky because the scriptural use of the word believer is more serious than my intention here. I would question the modern pattern of being a "believer" where we might believe in Jesus, go to church on Sunday, yet live Monday to Saturday with little concern for the demands of the gospel. Scripture says that even the demons believed. (James 2:19)

Discipleship

Discipleship is a discipline that involves instruction, study, correction and obedience to the Lord. It involves not only the initial conversion, but also learning "...to observe all that I have commanded you" (Matthew 28:20). (See Appendix C – Principles of Discipleship)

Discipleship for us includes pastoral care from brothers or sisters more experienced in the way of the Lord. It involves a measure of Christian environment, as well as having a number of models of Christian living that we can respect and aspire to.

"On Mission"

Described

Our mission involves evangelization and establishing communities throughout the world who will, in turn, evangelize and raise up trained and formed disciples living our way of life.

> "...and what you have heard from me before many witnesses entrust to faithful men who will be able to teach others also." 2 Timothy 2:2

Outreach

We support the mission with prayer, with finances, and with missionaries who join in the work. The Servants of the Word (our brotherhood) have been key catalysts in that work and they have been joined by other disciples regionally and internationally. Our regional community-building teams have supported communities at all stages. Our regional youth teams have helped and supported young Christians.

Thousands have given their lives to the Lord in these outreaches.

Mutual and Necessary Elements

Management Terms

Two pertinent modern management terms are:
1) Synergy:
- *A dynamic state in which combined action is favored over the sum of individual component actions.*
- *Behavior of whole systems unpredicted by the behavior of their parts taken separately.*

2) Symbiosis:
- *Close and often long-term interactions between different biological species.*
- *The living together of unlike organisms.*

A combination of Terms

To me, nothing better expresses a combining of necessary elements in a divine/human endeavor than "a community of disciples on mission". As with farming, multiple elements are necessary, but the Lord provides the growth (1 Corinthians 3:6). Christian community is made up of disciples who have mission as the natural expression of their maturity. Disciples are trained and formed in community life by older brothers and sisters with whom they may one day join in mission. Christian mission <u>requires</u> Christian disciples and is supported and served by the strength of community.

Mutual Importance

Each element (community, disciples, and mission) is necessary and mutually important. The Body of Christ needs all three. When one or another is over-emphasized, something is lost. When one is almost or entirely missing, it is "code blue".

As Steve Clark has often described, I may be able to function without one of my legs, but that is not the original intent, the original design. Many of our Christian churches suffer from the lack of community, the lack of discipleship, or the lack of mission. Some are even crippled. The Holy Spirit is healing some of these weaknesses and equipping us to stand.

"And his gifts were to be that some should be apostles, some prophets, some evangelists, some pastors and teachers, to equip the saints for the work of ministry, for building up the body of Christ, until we all attain to the unity of the faith and of the full knowledge of the Son of God, to mature manhood, to the measure of the stature of the fullness of Christ; so that we may no longer be children, tossed to and fro and carried about with every wind of doctrine, by the cunning of men, by their craftiness in deceitful wiles. Rather, speaking the truth in love, we are to grow up in every way into him who is the head, into Christ, from whom the whole body, joined and knit together by every joint with which it is supplied, when each part is working properly, makes bodily growth and upbuilds itself in love." Ephesians 4:11-16

THE FRUIT OF UNITY

In naming a discussion of the topic of unity, several titles could be used, and this springs from the similarities found in a set of words: unity, union, communion, and community. It is difficult to address the overall topic of community without drifting somewhere into a discussion of unity. The scriptures address unity in both specific and general terms, and in some cases, the <u>fruit</u> of unity.

Scriptures on Unity, Togetherness and Body Life

One of the most foundational scriptures addressing unity is found in Ephesians 1:9-10

> *"For he has made known to us in all wisdom and insight the mystery of his will, according to his purpose which he set forth in Christ as a plan for the fullness of time, to unite all things in him, things in heaven and things on earth."*

The importance of this scripture cannot be overestimated since it presents God's plan from before the foundation of the world.

> *"...even as he chose us in him <u>before the foundation of the world</u>." Ephesians 1:4*

We might say or hear someone saying, "I wonder what the Lord is doing?" In a broad way, at least, we have an answer; he is "uniting all things in Christ." Togetherness in worship supports God's plan; togetherness in mission supports God's plan. We do not always know exactly what the Lord is doing, but he has revealed his overall plans and purposes to those who want to live for Christ.

On the other hand, his enemies, the world, the flesh and the devil, are diligently working to divide us and to disintegrate individuals, families, groups, denominations and even cities and nations. The world and the flesh are used by the devil to create chaos, division and disintegration. God integrates; the devil disintegrates. God brings us together in life; the devil disintegrates, takes us apart in death. A decomposing corpse is the tapestry of his best work. The resurrected body, united with Jesus, is the work of the life, death and resurrection of Christ.

Good Fruit

"A healthy tree bears good fruit, but a poor tree bears bad fruit" (Matthew 7:17 Today's English Version). What does bad fruit look like? It looks like disunity, disintegration, and death. Of the Ten Commandments, the positive-sounding ("Thou shalt!") examples present behavior that unites. The negative-sounding ones ("Thou shalt not!") warn about behaviors that divide and disintegrate. Murder (and violence), stealing, adultery, lying and coveting all cause trouble and divide human groupings. So we see in all of this a *tool for discernment*: does my decision, or behavior, or action bring God's people closer together or further apart? Does my new house or new job mean more community? Or does it mean less community? Matthew 12:33c (Today's English Version) says, "A tree is known by the kind of fruit it bears."

Unity and Prayer

> *"Again I say to you, if two of you on earth agree about anything they ask, it will be done for them by my Father in heaven. For where two or three are gathered in my name, there am I in the midst of them." Matthew 18:19*

Some have said, "When two people agree about anything, it's already a miracle!" This scripture is at least stating that people gathered together (even two!) is God's plan for how we should intercede. It is often the case that sickness and calamity can have a unifying effect on God's people, as they gather to bring the Lord's power into a difficult or even impossible situation.

In my own family, when leukemia struck my grandson, all petty differences and disagreements suddenly were eclipsed by the need for unity in fasting and prayer which brought us closer together. Thirteen years later and defying all odds (including an episode with Ewing Sarcoma), he graduated from high school! Our family came together in prayer and we were joined by brothers and sisters in community, in the Sword of the Spirit worldwide, and in the broader church. One fruit of unity is power in prayer.

Signs of the Times

> *"He answered and said to them, "When it is evening you say, 'It will be fair weather, for the sky is red'; and in the morning, 'It will be stormy today, for the sky is red and threatening. You know how to interpret the appearance of the sky, but you cannot interpret the signs of the times. An evil and adulterous generation seeks for a sign, bu no sign shall be given to it except the sygn of Jonah" Matthew 16:2-4*

My wife and I love to watch the weather channel. For her, it is like a great adventure. "When Weather Changed History!" is one of her favorite shows. As a show, it symbolizes man's interaction with the supernatural: 1) we are immersed in it; 2) we ignore it at our peril; 3) it can bring both blessing and calamity; 4) it can be studied but not mastered; 5) you can run but you cannot hide; 6) man's machinations are subordinate to and far inferior to its power.

The weather can be embarrassing. At one time, I lived near our TV weatherman. One Sunday, while driving to church, I saw him shoveling four inches of "sunshine" (his prediction) out of his driveway. I tooted my horn and smiled in a pleasant (yet teasing) way.

On another occasion, I took two of my friends and their son out for a short boat ride on the lake. The wind came up and we never got out of the lagoon before we were swamped by the choppy water. Fortunately, it was only three or four feet deep and we were able to find their son who had slipped under the boat! I was (and still am) more embarrassed than the weatherman. Decades later, we are still friends and I have a much deeper boat!

The scripture verse warns that we can predict the weather but we cannot interpret the signs concerning these times. It warns that people can be evil and godless and yet ask for a miracle. To be evil and godless is often to be sinning against the Ten Commandments, against God's plan. His plan is to unite; the world the flesh and the devil are disobedient, divisive, and block the power of God for the miracle that is needed. Some hallmarks of our society are: negativity, slander, disobedience and division... godless evil.

So, to obey is to unite and usher in the power of God. To disobey is to divide people and to block the power of God.

Wait...Together

"And while staying with them he charged them not to depart from Jerusalem, but to wait for the promise of the Father, which he said, 'you heard from me...'" Acts 1:4

"When the day of Pentecost had come, they were all together in one place." Acts 2:1

Two of the most difficult things for modern, independent, individualistic people to do is to wait, and worse, to wait together. Our fast food culture teaches us that waiting is bad, fast is good. Doing it "my way" is better than doing it "our way." No one getting to tell me what to do is seen as better than being "bossed around." Even good leadership can be interpreted as "lording it over us." These postures or mindsets leave us hopelessly incapable of dealing with God who: 1) has tons of time on his hands; 2) wants to be together with us; 3) thinks that he is in charge of this family of his; and 4) thinks that he gets to decide how it is ordered. Because the first disciples were able to "wait...together," we have Pentecost, the birth of the Christian church.

Unity a Gift...to be Preserved

"Lead a life worthy of the calling to which you have been called, with all lowliness and meekness, forbearing one another in love, eager to maintain the unity of the Spirit in the bond of peace. There is one body and one Spirit, just as you were called to the one hope that belongs to your call." Ephesians 4:1-4

Clearly, unity is a gift of the Spirit, and it is a gift that we preserve and we maintain. We make decisions in our lives in a way that respects it and protects it. Again, we build in the little discernment test: Question: Does this decision yield more community (unity), or less community?

One Modern Approach to Scripture

"For I know the plans I have for you, says the Lord, plans for welfare and not for evil, to give you a future and a hope. Then you will call upon me and come and pray to me, and I will hear you. You will seek me and find me; when you seek me with all your heart, I will be found by you, says the Lord..." Jeremiah 29:11-13

A number of years ago, I had a long, serious, almost fatal battle with knee surgeries, infections, etc. My daughter, Jeanette, gave me a poster inscribed with the above scripture. It was quite encouraging hanging from the wall where I could see it from my bed. My friend, Bill, sent the same scripture to me in an e-mail assuring me that the Lord had more for me to do.

Another encouraging scripture that often gets a poster is Revelation 3:20: "Behold, I stand at the door and knock; if any one hears my voice and opens the door, I will come in to him and eat with him, and he with me."

Personal at the Expense of the Corporate

Most scriptures can have a beneficial, encouraging effect on the individual (as in my example above). Due to our great division, isolation, and individualism, we often personalize scriptures at the expense of the corporate. The scriptures cited were actually written to groups or to a people. In Jeremiah 29, verse 14 says "I will gather you in from all the nations." So it is not originally intended just for my bedroom wall! Revelation 3:20 (Today's English version) is written to the church at Laodicea...Christians! Verse 21 follows: "To those who win the victory, I will give the right to sit beside me on my throne." Verse 22 says, "Listen to what the Spirit says <u>to the churches</u>."

One more example: it is "**Our**" Father, not just "my" Father at the beginning of the Lord's Prayer. Keeping the sense of "our" in my prayer orientation has a joining and a uniting effect on the body of Christ. It deepens our awareness and appreciation of the familial nature of Christianity and diminishes the tendency to over-personalize and isolate the individual. Because of the culture we live in and the way we live (often isolated in our homes), it would be difficult to over-emphasize the corporate nature of Christianity and the unity that is at the heart of God's plan. There is something mysterious about unity and fruit as in Jesus' story about the farmer who plants a seed, does his part and then does not really understand why or how it grows (Mark 4:26-27).

God's plan, as scripture reveals, is corporate, with unity in Christ as its goal. Yet, it has personal effect, application, and responsibility.

The Fruit of Unity

The fruit of unity can be assessed and evaluated from different perspectives. For example, I can examine the fruit of Christian unity in my own life, my own spirituality, etc. I can also evaluate it based on how my personal life has affected other groupings, the Kingdom of God, or all of mankind. In the Fruit of Unity (Appendix B), different perspectives are intermingled in the rather long yet incomplete lists of fruit at the individual, family, community, regional, and international levels of our community life. The lists were compiled at a community forum of the People of God. That is to say, after 35 years of community life, we were stepping back to see what fruit we could see in our life together. The lists were compiled in a one hour session, and are not prioritized or defined. We will look at a few examples at each level, but it is worth noting that some of the identified fruit mentioned could be seen as "worthy of the investment" of time, money, etc.

Individual

At the personal level there are a number of things that could be listed under the heading of discipleship: self-knowledge, character formation, teaching, accountability, etc. These are noteworthy effects on the individual, whether married or single, and are specifically intended results of the way our community is structured: initiations courses, small groups, pastoral care, etc. The maturing of the Christian disciple is one of the main objectives.

This is a two-part process: there is maturity that we gain from simply receiving the teaching and training, and then there is a second level of maturity that comes from putting the principles into practice in loving and serving our brothers and sisters in the Lord, as well as advancing the Kingdom of God in the world.

The second level of maturity cannot be done for you by any leader or teacher, but must be personally engaged in to take effect. Sadly, many brothers and sisters level off after the first stage of maturity and never reap the full effects of Christian maturity that come from engaging the cross of service. In that sense, community life serves us by providing a good place for us to die to self. The phrase "a place to live, a place to die", describes these two levels of personal maturity.

Family

At the family level, marriage support, children (protecting the value of life), parenting support, peer support for kids, and understanding of the roles of husband/wife and mother/father are all significant fruits of community life. If we existed just to help marriages to stay together, it would be worth the investment.

For family life to have its full effect, children must have both levels of maturing presented above: 1) formation; and 2) dying into family life. Refusing the second step retards their maturity.

As with the individual, families are also invited to go beyond the first stages and "die into" the broader life and mission of the community. This approach for family life helps to keep the membrane of the nuclear family receptive to the nutrients and support that can flow into the family, protecting it from a self-centered stagnation.

Local Community

Because we stay together in unity, we are able to do things as a community that none of us can do separately: men's retreats, men's breakfasts, women's retreats, conferences, summer camp, community retreats, University Christian Outreach, Life in the Spirit courses, healing weeks, etc. Our unity produces fruit that is beneficial to us, to the wider church and to the world. As a group, we are a witness to the Lord, a reflection of the unity that has its root in the Trinity and is a gift of the Spirit (Ephesians 4:3). Additionally, our denominational life is supported as we celebrate weddings, baptisms, communions, etc.

As with the family, the local community also gets to serve and sacrifice at the regional level as we serve in trans-local community building, regional youth work, summer conferences, etc. Our local life and schedule are often disrupted for the good of serving and participating at the regional level.

International Level

Our North American region is one of the five regions that make up the Sword of the Spirit. The fruit of that international unity is first of all a bulwark: a community of communities that share a common way of life and a common mission. We are blessed with a global vision, teaching resources and courses, music gifts, mission trips, government, etc.

Final Comments and Summary

At the beginning of this chapter, I said that this could have several titles. One could be, "What happens when Christian individuals, families, clans and tribes stay together?" The answer is, "A lot!" (See Appendix B, The Fruit of Unity). Another title could be, "What happens when Christian people stay to themselves?" The answer is, "Far less."

Two Words

Our local community was initially inspired by two words from the Lord: 1) "Gather my people together;" and 2) "Build to last." The first word implies community or some kind of body and not just a threshold ministry. The second implies some kind of approach or order or structure that serves the ongoing unity. We have tried to do that and we think that the initial fruit identified encourages endurance and faithfulness to the call and mission.

Discipleship: A Change of Plans

One of the hallmarks of a disciple of Christ is his ability to handle "a change of plans." This shows up several times in the life of Joseph. He plans to "put Mary away" but is instructed in a dream to change his plans (Matthew1:20). He plans to stay in Bethlehem awhile but is told to flee to Egypt (Matthew 2:13). He plans to stay awhile in Egypt but is told to return to Israel (Matthew 2:20). We don't know a lot about Joseph, but we do know that he followed the Lord and that he could lead his family in obedience to the Lord. Who among us could ask his wife to take a trip to Egypt as a new mother (Matthew 2:14)?

Being gathered together in a way that lasts involves a life of changing our plans, first for the new disciple, then for the new Christian family, and finally for the mature disciples and Christian families. Simply said, "Our ways are not his ways;" "*Our plans are not his plans,*" and the sooner we realize that, the sooner we can move freely in the life of a mature disciple.

To See or Not to See

All of this having been said, it really does seem that *those who give the most get the most.* Those who die into the Lord's will get the most life. Those who see the most light and move toward the light seem to see even more clearly. Those who are most committed and determined to stay together seem to enjoy the most fruit of unity.

Evidentiary fruit

> *For the wrath of God is revealed from heaven against all ungodliness and wickedness of men who by their wickedness suppress the truth. For what can be known about God is plain to them, because God has shown it to them. Ever since the creation of the world his invisible nature, namely, his eternal power and deity, has been clearly perceived in the things that have been made So they are without excuse.*
> Romans 1:18-20

The Bible says that God's invisible qualities are perceived in the things that God has made. So, creation is *evidentiary* to the nature and existence of God. It is to be presented at the trial of the wicked and the godless. *We would say, in a similar way, that the fruit of unity is evidentiary to the power and presence of God in our midst.*

The Gap

Even though we see a gap between the ideal of Christian community and the reality of its human expression, the fruit is astounding! So, we must get over any differences that we may have, stay together and continue to produce fruit that is pleasing to the One who created us.

ANTICIPATING PURPOSE

In times of confusion or rapid change, it seems common to search for purpose. *The Purpose Driven Life* by Rick Warren, tapped into this strong current of underlying questioning and searching. Modern trends of gender-confusion, icon-bashing, and the pervasive challenge of authority have not led to more clarity, but to more confusion. One of the enemy's strongest strategies is to convince us that no one knows the truth. When I have eliminated all outside authorities and teachers, I am now my own expert. "I" must then have all the answers; and if I do not, I will get plenty of help from my ancient dark friend.

After more than 35 years of teaching, I have found the recent class of young adults to be mostly likely to take a posture of, "Who says so?" Yet at the same time a searching and questioning is in place. There is a recognized vulnerability that is the result of this new individualism. We can be like hungry children who are too "picky" to eat.

By "anticipating purpose" I mean to address something more than what is *my* purpose. In one grandiose sweep I would like to suggest that we try to anticipate and explore God's purposes, his intentions, and his patterns. As we understand his purposes, we can explore with increasing success, our own purposes. This would be a grand undertaking beyond the realm of human minds, so I'll limit myself to just a few examples.

The Work of Christ

The life and work of Christ is a grand topic that has been covered by many books (and gospels). His roles of teacher, healer, and deliverer have all been addressed. Each role has generated specific books such as, *The Teaching of Christ*, by Donald Wuerl.

He came to save us from the enemy; he came to save us from ourselves; he came to save us *for* the kingdom of heaven, for all time. To list all of the features of the work of Christ is beyond this chapter. But, I think there is a great value in looking at the question, "What was Jesus concerned about in his last free moments on earth?" The answer is *unity*

> *"I do not pray for these only, but also for those who believe in me through their word, that they may all be one; even as thou, Father, art in me, and I in thee, that they may also be in us, so that the world may believe that thou has sent me"*
> *John 17:20-21*

The Work of the Spirit

Assuming Jesus and the Holy Spirit to be on the same page, we can now anticipate one main purpose of the Holy Spirit: *unity*. Steve Clark in his article, "Baptism in the Holy Spirit and Community" says it simply, "Central to the work of the Holy Spirit is unity."[1]

> *"For he has made known to us in all wisdom and insight the mystery of his will, according to his purpose which he set forth in Christ as a plan for the fullness of time, to unite all things in him, things in heaven and things on earth." Ephesians 1:9-10*

Interestingly, unity is a gift of the Spirit, and, as with all the gifts, human beings are entrusted with it, having a responsibility to preserve it and use it well.

> *"Always seek to keep the unity which the Spirit gives." Ephesians 4:3 (New American Bible)*

In 1 Corinthians 12, gifts are listed with a certain descriptive caution: "As it is, there are many parts but one body" (verse 20). Again in 1 Corinthians 14:12 "Try above everything else to make greater use of those (gifts) which help to build up the church."

(Today's English Version) This whole section in 1 Corinthians 12-14 seems to be calling forth giftedness, but giftedness that is: 1) expressed together in groups; 2) exercised properly and in good order; and 3) upbuilds the *one* body.

These markers, these features of the last prayer of Christ and these descriptions of the gifted body by Paul allow us to predict, to anticipate to some extent, what Pentecost would be like. More importantly, it allows us to anticipate what *future* experiences of Pentecost (significant moves of the Spirit) would be like.

So here is a layman's first attempt at anticipating the purposes of the Holy Spirit: Pentecost will have unity as its purpose; Pentecost will be marked by unusual giftedness; Pentecost will have community as its result; Pentecost will create circumstances and experiences which will necessitate responsible and capable pastoral care.

The Seven-Step Pattern of the Holy Spirit's Work

If the last section was not adventurous enough, I will now try to identify a seven step pattern using the scriptural accounts that we have. This is not from some great theological authority. I have seven steps because in the Bible seven is considered a perfect number. You might study the same texts and come up with six or eleven. These are elements that I see in the verses. I am using them to explain and/or anticipate the purpose that the Lord has given us in community.

1) Obedience

Acts 1:4 says he commanded them to wait in Jerusalem. In one verse we have two things that modern people hate: commands and waiting. Not many people "wait on the Lord" anymore, but I think waiting or anticipating is one key. Waiting together is another (Acts 2:1). Also worth noting, obedience prepares us for power.

2) Worship

We know that some prayer was taking place; tradition supports that (Acts 1:24).

3) Pentecostal Power
Scripture says that there was a great noise like a violent wind. It was loud enough to gather a crowd.

4) Charisms or Gifts
"They were all filled with the Holy Spirit and began to speak in other tongues..."
Acts 2:4

5) Interior Change (zeal, courage, etc.)
Acts 2:14 Peter stood up with the eleven...
Acts 2:13 Some were mocking (not safe).
Acts 2:36 Peter accused (courage).
Acts 2:40 Peter warned and pleaded (zeal).

6) Evangelism
"About 3000 were added..." Acts 2:41
"Go therefore and make disciples of all nations..." Matthew 28:19-20

7) Community
"They devoted themselves to the apostles' teaching, and fellowship, to the breaking of bread and the prayers." Acts 2:42
"...breaking bread in their homes" Acts 2:46

Thus the first Christian community was the result of this first Pentecost. They did not disperse until later when persecution began: wherever they went, they then formed new communities.

Why Community?

Heaven is a grouping (see Revelation). It is almost always described in groups together ("with one voice") in unity, the work of the Holy Spirit. The New Testament community was that early, first, Christian example of the kingdom of God on earth. Subsequent eruptions of the Spirit would produce similar results. Works of God draw his people together; they worship and they courageously evangelize with power. That's just the way it is.

Reverse Implications of Anticipation: What is a Christian Community?

Ah, the joys of complicated titles. I once saw a hammer described as a Positional Adjustment Impact System! Apparently, this allows you to charge the government a higher purchase price!

I think the reverse implications that we might observe can help us to describe at least a sketch of Christian community.
- **Obedience:** A community obeys together and can be directed by the Lord as a body.
- **Worship:** A community worships the Lord together.
- **Pentecostal power:** A community experiences an empowering when it worships the Lord and listens to him.
- **Charismatic gifting:** Gifts flow from the worship of the Lord, and not just for one or a few anointed individuals.
- **Interior change:** There is an interior impact on the body of believers; postures and attitudes change when it worships together.
- **Evangelism:** The gospel is spread with zeal.
- **Community:** New life is welcomed and fostered; a way of life results. Christianity is something to do together, not just as isolated individuals. We are devoted to teaching, praying and spending time together. Family-like relationships grow. Pentecost results in community and it also defines it.

Acts 2:42 "Devoted to"

For the sake of this discussion, I would like to consider "devoted to" as a *power* statement. People can humanly be devoted to a set of things; but when they *suddenly* become devoted to a set of things, something mysterious, something powerful has happened.

Teaching

Of the Christian groups that I am familiar with, those who are baptized in the Spirit seem to have a remarkable devotion to teaching and to the study of scripture. I see this as a result of the Pentecostal experience. There is (for most) nothing flashy or attractive about teaching, yet we see a devotion to, an empowerment in the area of teaching (both giving and receiving). There seems to be an unusual understanding, appreciation and benefit from teaching.

Breaking of Bread

For most there is also a new understanding of, benefiting from, and appreciation for the Eucharist/Lord's Supper. This is often accompanied by a deeper appreciation of church ties and commitments.

Prayers

There is a remarkable new devotion to prayer, especially corporate prayers (initially) and eventually, individual prayer. Corporate prayer can be remarkably powerful and have been a great witness leading to repentance and conversion for many souls.

Fellowship

They were devoted to fellowship. They appreciated being together; they benefited from it.

EMPOWERED TO LIVE IN COMMUNITY

One of the first recorded results of Pentecost was the new church, the new community. Pentecost is seen as the birthday of the church, and the church is, at the beginning, a *community*. I use that word because of the way it is described in Acts: its "hallmarks" are community-like and it is not simply a worshiping congregation.

Some "hallmarks" of the early church:

1) It was different. It would be called "the Way" by outsiders. Outsiders would comment, "See how they love one another." They shared. (Acts 2:44-45)
2) Their contact and times together were frequent. "…day after day they met together as a group…" (Acts 2:44 Today's English Version)
3) It had a family look to it. They called each other brothers and sisters.
4) A rarely used word (agape) would be needed to describe their love of the brethren.
5) A strong word (koinonia) would be needed to describe their relationships.
6) They shared meals together.
7) Their families were centered in the family of God.

The Number One Grace of Pentecost

I believe that this early community was the #1 grace of Pentecost...this is your sign, this is your wonder, and this is your miracle: people loving one another in Christ and centering their lives in Him, in a common way of life.

To support this conclusion, I ask you to consider this: in 1 Corinthians 12-19, the various gifts are discussed and we have the "more excellent" way of love described in chapter 13. Various gifts are ranked and compared; prophesy is given a high place. These giftings or gifted persons are compared to being parts of a body: less noble parts, more beautiful parts, etc.

But, this whole discussion of "parts" *presupposes the body* and it insists that we upbuild the body with our gifts. Therefore, the number one grace or result of Pentecost is the body. All of the gifts and roles are in support of and for the up-building of the body. Gifts such as healing or prophecy should never be "stand alone" phenomena, but are a part of and an expression of the body. To wander the countryside prophesying misses the main intent of Pentecost: the body itself.

Koinonia: Spiritually Bonded Community

Many years ago, the great Christian teacher, Bob Mumford, tackled the topic of "koinonia". After five or six tapes with a number of quotes from Greek scholars, he still seemed at a loss to define the word "koinonia", which weakly translates as "fellowship" in Acts 2:42. There seems to be a spiritual bond that happens among those who are baptized in the Spirit. It seems mysterious and beyond our understanding...a bond of unity. We often notice a certain inner celebration when we are together. It can be noticed at retreats, summer camp, and Lord's Day celebrations. Children "catch" it at retreats, and we do ourselves and our children a disservice to miss these yearly events. It seems that the more the event is focused on the Lord, the more noticeable is the inner celebration and bonding.

This inner magnetism or grace can even have a regional or international expression as we gather with other members of the Sword of the Spirit at the summer conference or international leaders' events. Our children experience that bond at regional youth events, and, in a very real way, they understand our "vision and call" more by this experience of koinonia.

As a personal example, I have two friends, Jim and Connie, who live over 30 miles from me. We are in the People of God Community together, but we are from different locations, somewhat different geography, different families, different parishes, different social circles, and have different hobbies. Yet, when we are together something inside of me resonates, celebrates, and rejoices with them. My covenant with them acknowledges what is already there: a spiritual bonding in the Spirit: koinonia.

Our Response

Over the years, I think, it has been a mistake of the charismatic renewal to overly focus on the gifts and to miss this koinonia unity. It is a magnetism, yet it can be ignored if we walk away. The attraction can be broken or weakened by inattention. I believe the writer of Hebrews 10:25 warned about this when he said, "... not neglecting to meet together as is the habit of some."

We should nourish, stir to life, and protect the unity (Ephesians 4:3). We should *anticipate the purposes* of the Holy Spirit and we should adjust our decisions accordingly. (See Joseph's responses in Matthew 1:19&24, 2:14, and 2:19-23.)

We are first and foremost empowered to live in a local, worshiping, and directable people who will love God and one another in a common way of life. By doing so, we both anticipate and participate in the purposes of the Holy Spirit.

CLOSING COMMENTS

Before giving a summary, I want to give some closing comments in light of the issues raised and their likelihood or validity.

If you have very little background or experience with Christian communities, some of the concepts covered may seem Utopian, unrealistic or unlikely: trans-generational community, coherent living, daily life ecumenism, anticipating purpose, etc. If you are in a small community and not associated with any network of communities, you may have found certain chapters to be foreign to your local experience.

I want to assure the reader that in the Sword of the Spirit International, we do have quite a number of communities that have most or all of these elements in place—or nearly in place. There are some elements that work better for large communities than for small. It is also the case that if a large community is not aware of a needed approach, it may have little or no experience or success in that area of its life. For example, the vision to be trans-generational as a local community surfaced in North America in the early 1990's. At that time, we had a number of large communities around the world that had little or no success at retaining the younger members. It was not even an intention or an objective.

My local community began working to pass on our way of life to our children in the late 1980's. Recently, we celebrated the birth of our first fourth generation member! Additionally, we have over 40% of our membership that are second generation or their spouses. We are, however, on the smaller side with just around two hundred adults and children.

Trans-generational community life is more difficult for smaller communities since the number of youth is small and the ability to support outreach across the spectrum of ages and seasons is less than in a large community. Having programs and outreach for elementary, junior high, university and post-university requires a good number of staff persons.

Although larger communities find it easier to staff a large number of outreaches and ministries, they can run the risk of becoming activity-oriented, program-centered or machine-like. Members can develop an approach that relies on "professionals" to do the work of evangelism and mission. The larger communities can also run the risk of becoming de-personalized, and lose part of the heart of Christian community: personal relationships. Years ago, I served on a visitation to one of our smaller communities, Morningstar, in Jackson, Michigan. I discovered an extraordinary level of personal relationship, personal support and love of the brethren.

I do believe that smaller Sword of the Spirit communities can be trans-generational, especially if they start early, plan well, and make full use of the regional youth programs. I also believe that larger Sword of the Spirit communities can maintain high levels of personal relationship with a growing use of clusters, and a close attention to the smaller parts of the community: districts and small groups.

So, communities large and small can have some or all of these elements in place. The development or degree of effectiveness can vary from just beginning to work, to that of a very well established reality.

Whether large or small, some balance of maintenance and mission is needed, along with an informed leadership that diligently and vigilantly moves things forward in a way that makes sense and bears fruit.

SUMMARY AND CONCLUSIONS

1) Many Christian church bodies and local churches are not effective, or they are not as effective as they should be in expressing all that the Scripture reveals.
2) The changes in world cultures due to the industrial revolution, the enlightenment, etc. have wreaked havoc on the church, human relationships, families and the various expressions of "natural" community.
3) Societal indicators[1] point to a serious decline in many major cultures. That is to say, the modern expressions of cultural evolution have not helped society, but have wounded it, perhaps mortally.
4) The present state of things in the world and in our Christian churches should not be seen as "business as usual" but "code blue".[2]
5) Most Christians should be motivated to try something... anything!
6) The present state of things is beyond man's ability to repair. It is a moral, societal free fall.
7) Christianity should be basically expressed as a love of God and a love of neighbor.
8) The Holy Spirit has been actively responding to the need, raising up movements and new communities as a part of the solution.

9) These movements and communities have great individual impact, and they are also meant to bring renewal to the church and reform to society. They <u>advance</u> the Kingdom of God.
10) Under the influence of the Holy Spirit, the evolution of these movements and communities tends to be toward discipleship and mission.
11) These movements and new communities offer a certain hope, if they are lived in a fully committed way: a deepening discipleship and a growing sense of mission.
12) Some local expressions have developed into national or international .networks. Our Sword of the Spirit has formed an international bulwark of the Christian faith.
13) The gospel will be preached, individuals will encounter Christ, new converts will be discipled in the ways of Christ, the mission will grow, and the Christian way of life will be a lamp on a stand, a city on a hill.
14) The Father wants a family and we will continue to grow it until we die. That's a big part of what it means to be Christ-like, Christian.
15) We in the Sword of the Spirit hope to make a contribution to the ongoing renewal of the church.

FOOTNOTES

Introduction
[1] Appendix H: The People of God: a Snapshot
[2] Appendix G: Resource Reading List

Community and the Nature of Church
[1] "Code blue": a medical term for an emergency situation; it is also intended to call into action a team of life savers and the equipment needed to save a life.

Vision
[1] Our Sunday Visitor, November 15, 2009
[2] The premise of this book

The Three Greatest Needs of the Christian Church
[1] Note: There are denominational differences about the "born again" experience versus the salvation reality which some say takes place at baptism, others at accepting Christ. There are sacramental and experiential differences and emphases.

[2] The Theological Locus of Ecclesial Movements (resource TL), Cardinal Joseph Ratzinger, 1998; p. 1, para.1

[3] On Ecclesial Movements and New Communities (resource M), Cardinal Rylko, Zenit Weekly News Analysis, April 1, 2006; section 3, para. 6

[4] Ibid, section 1, para. 1

[5] Ibid, section 3, para. 7

Models of Life A
¹Barna Group Study,©. Worldnetdaily.com, March 3, 2005

Models of Life B
¹Larry Badaczewski, Perspectives, June 20, 2004
²Richard Rohr, Greek Society
³Webster's New World Dictionary, World Publishing Co. ©. 1953
⁴Larry Badaczewski, Perspectives, June 20, 2004
⁵Barna Group Study, © Worldnetdaily.com, March 3, 2005

A Catholic Apologetic for Community
¹TheTheological Locus of Ecclesial Movements, Cardinal Ratzinger, 1998
² On Ecclesial Movements and New Communities, Cardinal Rylko, Zenit Weekly News Analysis, April 1, 2006

A Protestant Apologetic for Covenant Community
¹Toward a Protestant Rationale for Covenant Community, Paul C. Dinolfo, 2006
²The Two Structures of God's Redemptive Mission, Ralph D. Winter, August, 1973

Ecumenism
¹Ut Unum Sint Encyclical, Pope John Paul II
²Vatican City (Asia News) January 25, 2007

Covenant Christian Community
¹Catholic Times: 5/18/2003 Vol. 52: 31

Anticipating Purpose
¹Baptism in the Holy Spirit and Community, Steve Clark, Pentecost Today, July/August/September 2008

Summary and Conclusion
¹Right from Wrong, Josh McDowell and Bob Hostetler, Chapter 1: A Generation in Crisis; ©Word Publishing 1994
²"Code blue": a medical term for an emergency situation; it is also intended to call into action a team of life savers and the equipment needed to save a life.

APPENDICES

A. Definitions

B. The Fruit of Unity

C. Some Core Principles of Discipleship

D. Decisions that Impact our Trans-generational Vision

E. Covenant of the People of God

F. Covenant Scriptures

G. Resource Reading List

H. The People of God: a Snapshot

Appendix A:
DEFINITIONS

Baptism in the Spirit: The experience of being immersed in the Spirit and of being open to his spiritual gifts. Prayer for this release of the Spirit happens somewhere in the Life in the Spirit course, commonly in the fifth session. Many receive the gift of tongues, prophecy, a love of scripture or some other sign or charismatic gift. Other gifts may follow later as a part of life in the body. The gifts are primarily meant for the wider body (see 1 Corinthians 12 and 14) and pre-suppose its existence. Some, such as the gift of tongues, also have a deeply personal application as in daily prayer life.

Charismatic Renewal: At the beginning of the twentieth century, there was a Pentecostal visitation among some free-church Protestants. That "Baptism in the Spirit" led to modern experiences of spiritual gifts such as tongues, prophecy, etc. That outpouring eventually visited denominational churches, including the Episcopalians and the Catholics by the 1960's. Those (most folks) who stayed in their churches, but met in prayer meetings (usually ecumenical) to exercise the gifts were called neo-Pentecostals or simply Charismatics.

Cluster: Some members live in clusters or neighborhoods where homes are on the same street or where back yards connect. If the children can easily get to the homes in the cluster, the likelihood of intersecting or overlapping of life experiences increases. Living in a cluster does not guarantee a higher level of the sharing of life; it just provides the possibility of increasing our life together. Those with isolationist life patterns or out-of-control schedules might be just as unavailable across the street as across town. Sometimes clusters schedule prayer times, celebrations, desserts, or Lord's Day celebrations, in order to increase their time together. Good relationships can become very strong after years of living close together.

Community: For the sake of this writing, "community" is intended to mean a network of intentional relationships of members who are seeking a common way of life together. It is not just a functional use of the word as in "banking" community or the "marketing" community. It is not here used in the recreation or activity applications: the racing community or the boating community. Rather, it is used to describe individuals who band together in response to a call to be a people.

Community Care: All of the elements available in community life that contribute to the present and ongoing care and development as a disciple: pastoral care, teaching, courses, worship gatherings, small groups, etc.

Coordinator: A member of the male leadership council or coordinators' council of each community. The coordinators' council is normally presided over by the senior coordinator elected or ratified by the full members of the community.

Covenant: For Christian communities, a written agreement listing elements meant to describe the intended relationship among members and, as a people, with the Lord. It is an attempt to summarize the relational qualities expected of a disciple of Jesus Christ, usually extracted from the New Testament.

Discipleship: Initially, the process of growing from a new convert to a formed, mature disciple (student, follower) of Jesus. Longer term, it is the ongoing process of continued growth, development, and deepening conversion to the "mind of Christ". The first stage averages 3-5 years. Long term discipleship is life-long and includes training and development appropriate to the vocations and stages (ages and seasons) of life.

Ecumenism: A convergent, cooperative attempt to work together in mutual respect across denominational lines. A recognition of what all Christians have in common while respecting the differences and distinctions of denominational beliefs.

Life in the Spirit Seminar: A short course meant to lead folks to "decide for Christ," receive the baptism in the Spirit, and to become a disciple in the Body of Christ.

Lord's Day Celebrations: A group of prayers, sometimes including songs, that are said as part of a common meal or dessert time by families or groups of families and/or single members that honor the Lord and celebrate the opening of the Christian Sabbath on Saturday night, or some time on Sunday as a closing celebration. Can include discussion on Scriptural readings and entertainment.

Pastoral Care: The personal care and concern given to community members; each member has a pastoral leader, yet receives pastoral care in broader ways by other pastoral workers, community teaching, coordinator(s), and the common way of life.

Prophecy: Inspirations and "words from the Lord" that are sensed either in prayer or apart from prayer. There are many types of prophecies: encouragement, directional, predictive, etc. These inspirations or "words" do not replace or violate scripture and they are normally discerned within the group or within the meeting in which they are received. More serious prophecies require more careful discernment. Prophecy proceeds from the Baptism in the Spirit, but not all have a prophetic gift.

Initiations: The introductory and early formation period for new members. The teachings given will cover basic Christian truths, community life, relationships, etc. Pastoral care is heightened at this time as a new member experiences new ideas and new challenges. Typically, it is a period of rapid growth and change.

Senior Women Leaders: Each community has one or more senior women leaders (SWL). Several SWLs working together in a community might be called a senior women leaders' council or a senior women leaders' team. They have recognized pastoral and leadership gifts and often give assistance to the women who lead small groups.

Servants of the Word: A brotherhood of the Sword of the Spirit that is ecumenical, worldwide, and has a high degree of common life together. It has made and continues to make key contributions to Sword of the Spirit government, training, music and youth work. Steve Clark, its founder, is also founder of the Sword of the Spirit.

Small Groups: Small groups in the Sword of the Spirit are normally made up of 4-6 men or 4-6 women. Each group has a leader and the leader is usually (not always) the pastoral leader for each of the members. Small groups are for a regular (weekly or bi-weekly) sharing of life, needs for prayer, needs for counsel and input, etc. It is also a place for some accountability. The small group and the small group leader are important elements of the community care that we all receive in Christian community.

Sword of the Spirit: An international "community of communities:" a network of communities having a common way of life. Some communities are denominational in membership and in some elements of spirituality (e.g. Catholic), but all are ecumenically convergent—fostering a respect and acceptance of Christians from other denominations. The Sword of the Spirit has a charismatic spirituality, and traces its roots to the Charismatic Renewal which flourished in the 1960's and 1970's. The resulting spirituality has evangelical and Pentecostal elements.

Visitations: Each full member community has a visitation approximately every five years. Communities in formation have visitations more frequently, perhaps every 2-3 years. The visitation team is made up of senior leaders from other communities. The purposes of a visitation are: to assist the local leaders in evaluating the community life, to identify potential growth areas, to surface/identify potential problems, to assess the local community's adherence to its intended and agreed-upon way of life, to be of any assistance requested by the coordinators council in exploring specific areas, and to give the local members an "outside ear" about any issues and concerns they may have. (Note: There is an outside coordinator who also assists in some of these purposes in an ongoing way.) Visitations are commonly 3-4 days, but would be longer or shorter depending on the purpose and need, as well as regional variations in approaches. A visitation report summarizes the team's observations for the members, the coordinators and the senior women leaders.

Appendix B:
THE FRUIT OF UNITY

Individual
- Character formation
- Love for the Lord
- Deeper prayer life
- Dependability
- Affirmation
- Correction
- Pastoral care/direction
- Fellowship
- Long-term stable relationships
- Self-knowledge
- Crisis support
- Understanding God's Word
- Prayer for healing
- Prophetic direction
- Support for life purpose
- Courtship support
- Accountability
- Singles inclusion in family life
- Trans-generational relating
- Personal balance
- Service opportunities
- Repentance/reconciliation
- Discovering gifts
- Learning

Teaching
Moral rectitude
Humility

Family
Children
Husband/wife meetings
Christian worldview
Peer support for kids
Roles of men/women
Roles of father/mother
Long-term friendships
Babysitting service
Financial advice
Lord's Day
Family prayer time support
Holiday/birthday celebrations
House projects
Sharing of goods
Denominational support
Retreats
Godparents
Manual labor support
Household living
Marriage support
Parenting support
Role models for children
Eldercare support
Conflict resolution
Family order
Cluster life
Support for kids at school

Local Community
Covenant commitment
Campout
Disaster relief support
Summer Camp
Cluster life celebrations/events
Opportunities to evangelize

Men's breakfast
Child care
Retreats
Witnessing
Social opportunities
Foundation talks
Support to larger events
Koinonia group
Unity
Transgenerational building
Using charismatic gifts
Hospitality
Purpose in life
Crafts
Vocational discernment
Understanding denominations
Leadership order
Employment connections
Baptisms, communions, confirmations, graduations
Charismatic gatherings
Forums
Leadership training
Men's/women's groups
University Christian Outreach
Men's house/women's house
Brotherhood/sisterhood parties
Summer prayer meetings
Life in the Spirit seminars
Youth groups
Support/service to churches
Community projects
Project help
Sword of the Spirit membership
Community conferences
Ecumenical witness
Sharing natural gifts & talents
Sharing resources/money
Sense of belonging

March for Life
Borrowing resources
Relationships among children
Cmty. birthday celebration
Vacations
Sports/leisure activities
Lord's Day
Sharing meals
Moral teaching and values
Good clean fun
People of God webpage

Regional (North American)
Visitations
Unified voice
Hospitality
Music
Summer Camp
University Christian Outreach
Mission trips
Courtship
Collegial leadership
Printed resources
GAP Program
Senior GAP Program
Summer Internship Program
Our body of teaching
YLD (Youth Leadership Development)
Women's leadership team
NARC (North American Regional Council)
Community building
Discipleship development
Common prophetic call
Translocal validation
Leadership formation
Job market/opportunities
Summer Conference
Inter-community relationships

Vision for missions
High school youth retreats
Winter Academy
Campus Outreach Academy
Spring Branding
Ranch Challenge
Boundary Water Trip
Christian Youth Challenge
Extended friendships/adults
Extended friendships/youth
Ecumenism
Detroit Summer Outreach
Outside coordinator
Brotherhood
Community development
Common vision
Potential marriage partners
Sharing resources
Spiritual resources
Bereavement support

International

Servants of the Word
GAP (year of service for college-age folks)
Sisterhood
International Mtg. for Singles
Being a bulwark:
Learning other languages and cultures
Global vision
Intl. Coordinators' Meetings
Senior Women's gatherings
Teaching/teaching resources
Music
Financial support
Common way of life
Vacation spots
Government
Vision for missions

Statement of Community Order
Sword of the Spirit history
Community Building Team
Establishing new communities
Wisdom
Miracles
Baptism in the Spirit
International conferences
Common vision
Ecumenical contribution
Hospitality
Global identity
Extended friendships
Strengthening commitments
Crisis support
Conflict resolution
Constitution
Establishing order
Church relations
Documents
Courses
International Ecumenical Youth Congress
International website
Living Bulwark Newsletter
Leadership resources
The arts
Authors
International e-mail
University Outreaches
Unity
Discerning God's will

SOME CORE PRINCIPLES OF DISCIPLESHIP

1) At the time of Jesus, the crowds were made up of apostles, disciples, believers, on-lookers, officials and enemies.

2) All Christians are called to be disciples. (Matthew 28:19)

3) Most worthwhile pursuits require some initiations/training to begin.

4) Most worthwhile pursuits require ongoing training to continue successfully.

5) To varying degrees, discipleship and training are lifetime pursuits.

6) There are multiple stages of life.

7) There is much natural and spiritual wisdom appropriate to the various stages and challenges of life.

8) God has a plan for my life.

9) The devil has a plan for my life.

10) There is much to learn at each of the stages of life to embrace God's plan and thwart the devil's plan.

11) Discipleship involves several elements: the disciple, the pastoral leader, the community, the scriptures, the Sword of the Spirit, and the Holy Spirit.

12) Improving any of the elements of discipleship can help the process to succeed.

13) Personal attitudes and posture are critical to the progress. Am I: teachable? correctible? arrogant? superior? critical? hopeful? weak of character? selfish? positive? negative? individualistic? addictive?

14) Faithfulness and commitment are crucial qualities. (Whimsical "Seinfeld" people will get nowhere).

15) Kingdom and societal roles are important to the Lord and His order. They give us regular opportunities to either rebel or humbly subordinate our wills, taming the flesh. (Ephesians 4:11, Hebrews 13:17, Colossians 3:18-20, 1 Timothy 5, 1 Peter 2:13-17)

16) You are fundamentally responsible for your own life.

17) There are no guarantees about how you will turn out.

18) We are a community of disciples on mission.

19) We believe that Christ has called Christians to be much more than they have been: for Christ, for themselves, and for the world.

Appendix D:
DECISIONS THAT IMPACT OUR TRANS-GENERATIONAL VISION

I. Three major approaches that affect our trans-generational vision
    A. Approach to dating and courtship
    B. Choice of college (location)
    C. Selecting a spouse
    Note: these can suddenly derail an otherwise good approach

II. Very high impact
    A. College/career/military decisions
    B. Living in the dorms
    C. Living away from home on a non-University Christian Outreach campus
    D. Allowing dating in high school
    E. Requiring attendance at community gatherings, events, socials, youth functions
    F. Driver's license/car access: limits of radius and personal use
    G. Amount of earnings parents allow youth to keep as spending/pocket money
    H. Degree of media access: amount and types of music, books, TV and movies
    I. The decision to live in a large cluster

III. Slow, steady, but certain impact
   A. Time spent in mixed settings: school, youth groups, "hanging out"
   B. Family order: mealtimes together, Lord's Day celebrations, etc.
   C. Curfew: time set, accountability
   D. Telephone access/text messages
   E. Time spent at work/job
   F. Modesty of speech, behavior, dress, and makeup
   G. Parents' unity regarding raising the children (and avoiding open arguments)
   H. Activities at school: number of groups, frequency of meeting, intensity of commitment required to participate
   I. Decisions that support community relationship building, not just with youth, but across the spectrum, including family-to-family relationships
   J. Young couples' school events: dances, banquets, proms
   K. Attending concerts on a regular basis (note: while negative element concerts are an obvious problem, excessive entertainment of any sort creates additional concerns)
   L. Allowing the development of an "I must be entertained" condition
   M. Parents' speech in front of children needs to be a positive experience of the Lord, their church, and the community (if too negative, erodes commitment of all involved)

COVENANT OF THE PEOPLE OF GOD

"This is the covenant that I will make with the house of Israel after those days, says the Lord: I will put my laws into their minds, and I will write them on their hearts, and I will be their God, and they shall be my people." Hebrews 8:10

Father, we recognize and accept the covenant to which you have called us. Jesus, we accept your lordship in our lives, we accept your call to be disciples and your commission to teach and make disciples of all people. Holy Spirit, we dedicate ourselves to allowing you to sanctify us, to work the Father's will in us, to form us as individuals into what we were meant to be, and to form us into a people of God. You have destroyed our isolation and have joined us together.

Faithful to our churches and to our primary vows such as marriage, we commit ourselves to each other as brothers and sisters in the Lord, entrusting our lives to him and to each other in him. We promise to build up, exhort, admonish, and to listen to one another, to communicate or call for help when we have a need, to be quick to forgive and to ask forgiveness, and to be a mutual support to each other. We commit ourselves to: loving one another as brothers and sisters in Christ, to faithfulness to our commitments, to regular community prayer, daily prayers, fellowship, teaching, and to our financial responsibility to the community. We agree to recognize the authority of the coordinators; and we agree to support, to pray for, and to submit to them. We will foster the growth of the community by supporting the programs of Christian initiation and formation in community life.

We recognize that by virtue of our membership in The People of God we are also members of The Sword of the Spirit, an international community of communities. We commit ourselves to love and support our brothers and sisters in The Sword of the Spirit throughout the world, and to serve with them in common mission.

We agree to be held to this covenant and to hold one another to it; we regard this as a serious commitment which we enter prayerfully.

Once we were no people, but now we are God's people.

COVENANT SCRIPTURES

Genesis 9:9 Behold, I establish my covenant with you and your descendants after you.

Genesis 9:12 And God said, "This is the sign of the covenant which I make between me and you and every living creature that is with you, for all future generations…"

Genesis 17:2 And I will make my covenant between me and you, and will multiply you exceedingly.

Genesis 17:7 And I will establish my covenant between me and you and your descendants after you throughout their generations for an everlasting covenant, to be God to you and to your descendants after you.

Genesis 17:9 And God said to Abraham, "As for you, you shall keep my covenant, you and your descendants after you throughout their generations."

Genesis 31:44 Come now, let us make a covenant, you and I; and let it be a witness between you and me.

Exodus 2:24 And God heard their groaning, and God remembered his covenant with Abraham, with Isaac, and with Jacob.

Exodus 19:5 Now therefore, if you will obey my voice and keep my covenant, you shall be my own possession among all peoples; for all the earth is mine.

Exodus 24:7 Then he took the book of the covenant, and read

it in the hearing of the people, who answered, "All that the Lord has spoken we will do, and we will be obedient."

Exodus 34:10 And he said, "Behold, I make a covenant. Before all people I will do marvels, such as have not been wrought in all the earth or in any nation; and all the people among whom you are shall see the work of the Lord; for it is a terrible thing that I will do with you."

Leviticus 26:9 And I will have regard for you and make you fruitful and multiply you, and confirm my covenant with you.

Deuteronomy 4:31 ...for the Lord your God is a merciful God; he will not fail you or destroy you or forget the covenant with your fathers which he swore to them.

Deuteronomy 5:3 Not with our fathers did the Lord make this covenant, but with us, who are all of us here alive this day.

Deuteronomy 7:9 Know therefore that the Lord your God is God, the faithful God who keeps covenant and steadfast love with those who love him and keep his commandments, to a thousand generations...

Deuteronomy 7:12 And because you hearken to these ordinances, and keep and do them, the Lord your God will keep with you the covenant and the steadfast love which he swore to your fathers to keep...

Deuteronomy 29: 9 Therefore be careful to do the words of this covenant that you may prosper in all that you do.

Deuteronomy 29:12 ...that you may enter into the sworn covenant of the Lord your God, which the Lord your God makes with you this day.

Deuteronomy 29:14 Nor is it with you only that I make this sworn covenant...

1 Samuel 18:3 Then Jonathan made a covenant with David, because he loved him as his own soul.

1 Samuel 23:18 And the two of them made a covenant before the Lord; David remained at Horesh, and Jonathan went home.

1 Kings 8:23 ...and said, "O Lord, God of Israel, there is no God like thee, in heaven above or on earth beneath, keeping covenant and showing steadfast love to thy servants who walk before thee with all their heart..."

(New American Bible) ...he said, "Lord, God of Israel, there is no God like you in heaven above or on earth below; you keep your covenant of kindness with your servants who are faithful to you with their whole heart."

2 Kings 13:23 (New American Bible) But the Lord was merciful with Israel and looked on them with compassion because of his covenant with Abraham, Isaac, and Jacob. He was unwilling to destroy them or to cast them out from his presence.

2 Kings 17:15 They despised his statutes, and his covenant he made with their fathers, and the warnings which he gave them. They went after false idols, and became false, and they followed the nations that were around them, concerning whom the Lord had commanded them that they should not do like them.

(New American Bible) They rejected his statutes, the covenant which he had made with their fathers, and the warnings which he had given them. The vanity they pursued, they themselves became: they followed the surrounding nations whom the Lord had commanded them not to imitate.

2 Kings 17:38 …and you shall not forget the covenant that I have made with you. You shall not fear other gods…

(New American Bible) The covenant which I made with you, you must not forget; you must not venerate other gods.

2 Kings 23:3 And the king stood by the pillar and made a covenant before the Lord, to walk after the Lord and to keep his commandments and his testimonies and his statutes, with all his heart and soul, to perform the words of this covenant that were written in this book; and all the people joined in the covenant.

1 Chronicles 16:15 He is mindful of his covenant forever, of the word that he commanded, for a thousand generations…

(New American Bible) He remembers forever his covenant which he made binding for a thousand generations…

2 Chronicles 6:14 …and said, "O Lord, God of Israel, there is no God like thee, in heaven or on earth, keeping covenant and showing steadfast love to thy servants who walk before thee with all their heart."

(New American Bible) Thus he prayed: "Lord, God of Israel, there is no God like you in heaven or on earth; you keep your covenant and show steadfast love to your servants who walk before thee with all their heart…"

2 Chronicles 15:12 And they entered into a covenant to seek the Lord, the God of their fathers, with all their heart and with all their soul.

2 Chronicles 21:7 Yet the Lord would not destroy the house

of David, because of the covenant he had made with David, and since he had promised to give a lamp to him and to his sons forever.

2 Chronicles 23:16 And Jehoiada made a covenant between himself and all the people and the king that they should be the Lord's people.

2 Chronicles 34:32 (New American Bible) He thereby committed all who were of Jerusalem and Benjamin, and the inhabitants of Jerusalem conformed themselves to the covenant of God, the God of their fathers.

Nehemiah 1:5 And I said, "O Lord God of heaven, the great and terrible God who keeps covenant and steadfast love with those who love him and keep his commandments…"

(New American Bible) I prayed, "O Lord, God of heaven, great and awesome God, you who preserve your covenant of mercy toward those who love you and keep your commandments…"

Psalm 25:10 All the paths of the Lord are steadfast love and faithfulness, for those who keep his covenant and his testimonies.

(New American Bible) All the paths of the Lord are faithful love toward those who honor the covenant demands

Psalm 25:14 The friendship of the Lord is for those who fear him, and he makes known to them his covenant.

(New American Bible) The counsel of the Lord belongs to the faithful; the covenant instructs them

Psalm 50:50 Gather to me my faithful ones, who made a covenant with me by sacrifice!

(New American Bible) Gather my faithful ones before me, those who made a covenant with me by sacrifice.

Psalm 74:20 Have regard for thy covenant; for the dark places of the land are full of the habitations of violence.

(New American Bible) Look to your covenant, for the land is filled with gloom; the pastures with violence.

Psalm 78:37 (New American Bible) Their hearts were not constant toward him; they were not faithful to his covenant.

Psalm 89:3 Thou hast said, "I have made a covenant with my chosen one, I have sworn to David my servant…"

Psalm 89:28 My steadfast love I will keep for him forever, and my covenant will stand firm for him.

Psalm 89:34 I will not violate my covenant or alter the word that went forth from my lips.

Psalm 105:8 He is mindful of his covenant forever, of the

word that he commanded, for a thousand generations.

Psalm 106:45 For their sake he remembered his covenant, and relented according to the abundance of his steadfast love.

Psalm 111:5 He provides food for those who fear him; he is ever mindful of his covenant.

Psalm 111:9 He sent redemption to his people; he has commanded his covenant for ever. Holy and terrible is his name!

(New American Bible) You sent deliverance to your people, ratified your covenant forever; holy and awesome is your name.

Psalm 132:12 If your sons keep my covenant and my testimonies which I shall teach them, their sons also for ever shall sit upon your throne.

(New American Bible) If your sons observe my covenant, the laws I shall teach them, their sons, in turn shall sit forever on your throne.

Isaiah 28:15 The earth lies polluted under its inhabitants; for they have transgressed the laws, violated the statutes, broken the everlasting covenant.

Isaiah 42:6 I am the Lord, I have called you in righteousness, I have taken you by the hand and kept you; I have given you as a covenant to the people, a light to the nations.

(New American Bible) I, the Lord, have called you for the victory of justice, I have grasped you by the hand; I have formed you, and set you as a covenant of the people, a light for the nations…

Isaiah 49:8 Thus says the Lord: "In a time of favor I have answered you, in a day of salvation I have helped you; I have kept you and given you as a covenant to the people, to establish the land, to apportion the desolate heritages.

Isaiah 54:10 For the mountains may depart and the hills be removed, but my steadfast love shall not depart from you, and my covenant of peace shall not be removed, says the Lord, who has compassion on you.

Isaiah 55:3 Incline your ear and come to me; hear, that your soul may live; and I will make you an everlasting covenant, my steadfast, sure love for David.

(New American Bible) Come to me heedfully; listen, that you may have life. I will renew you with the everlasting covenant, the benefits assured to David.

Isaiah 56:6 And the foreigners who join themselves to the

Lord, to minister to him, to love the name of the Lord, and to be his servants, everyone who keeps the Sabbath, and does not profane it, and holds fast my covenant...

(New American Bible) And the foreigners who join themselves to the Lord, ministering to him, loving the name of the Lord, and becoming his servants – all who keep the Sabbath free from profanation, and hold to my covenant...

Isaiah 59:21 And as for me, this is my covenant with them, says the Lord: My spirit which is upon you and my words which I have put in your mouth, shall not depart our of your mouth, or out of the mouths of your children, or out of the mouth of your children's children, says the Lord, from this time forth and for evermore.

(New American Bible) This is the covenant with them which I myself have made, says the Lord: My spirit which is upon you and my words that I have put in your mouth, shall never leave your mouth, nor the mouths of your children, nor the mouths of your children's children from now on and forever, says the Lord.

Jeremiah 11:3 You shall say to them: Thus says the Lord, the God of Israel: Cursed be the man who does not heed the words of this covenant.

(New American Bible) ...saying to them: Thus says the Lord, the God of Israel: Cursed be the man who does not observe the terms of this covenant...

Jeremiah 11:8 Yet they did not obey or incline their ear, but every one walked in the stubbornness of his evil heart. Therefore I brought upon them all the words of this covenant, which I commanded them to do, but they did not.

(New American Bible) But they did not listen or give ear, but every one walked in the stubbornness of his evil heart, till I brought upon them all the threats of this covenant which they had failed to observe as I commanded them.

Jeremiah 31:31 Behold, the days are coming, says the Lord, when I will make a new covenant with the house of Israel and the house of Judah.

(New American Bible) The days are coming, says the Lord, when I will make a new covenant with the house of Israel and the house of Judah.

Jeremiah 31:33 But this is the covenant which I will make with the house of Israel after those days, says the Lord: I will put my law within them, and I will write it upon their hearts; and I will be their God and they shall be my people.

(New American Bible) But this is the covenant which I will make with the house of Israel after those days, says the Lord: I will place my law within them, and write it upon their hearts; I will be their God, and they shall be my people.

Jeremiah 32:40 I will make with them an everlasting covenant, that I will not turn away from doing good to them; and I will put the fear of me in their hearts, that they may not turn from me.

(New American Bible) I will make with them an eternal covenant, never to cease doing good to them; into their hearts I will put the fear of me, that they may never depart from me.

Ezekiel 16:62 I will establish my covenant with you, and you shall know that I am the Lord.

(New American Bible) For I will re-establish my covenant with you, that you may know that I am the Lord.

Ezekiel 37:26 I will make a covenant of peace with them; it shall be an everlasting covenant with them; and I will bless them and multiply them, and will set my sanctuary in the midst of them for evermore.

(New American Bible) I will make with them a covenant of peace; it shall be an everlasting covenant with them, and I will multiply them, and put my sanctuary among them forever.

Daniel 9:4 I prayed to the Lord my God and made confession, saying, "O Lord, the great and terrible God, who keepest covenant and steadfast love with those who love him and keep his commandments…"

(New American Bible) I prayed to the Lord, my God, and confessed, "Ah, Lord, great and awesome God, you who keep your merciful covenant toward those who love you and observe your commandments…"

Malachi 2:10 Have we not all one father? Has not one God created us? Why then are we faithless to one another, profaning the covenant of our fathers?

Malachi 2:14 You ask, "Why does he not?" Because the Lord was witness to the covenant between you and the wife of your youth, to whom you have been faithless, though she is your companion and your wife by covenant.

Malachi 3:1 Behold, I send my messenger to prepare the way before me, and the Lord whom you seek will suddenly come to his temple; the messenger of the covenant in whom you delight, behold he is coming, says the Lord of hosts.

Sirach 17:12 He established with them an eternal covenant, and showed them his judgments.

Sirach 28:7 Remember the commandments, and do not be angry with your neighbor; remember the covenant of the Most High, and overlook ignorance.

Sirach 39:8 He will reveal instruction in his teaching, and will glory in the law of the Lord's covenant.

1 Maccabees 2:20 Yet I and my sons will live by the covenant of our fathers.

1 Maccabees 2:50 Now, my children, show zeal for the law, and give your lives for the covenant of our fathers.

Luke 1:72 …to perform the mercy promised to our fathers, and to remember his holy covenant…

(New American Bible) …to show mercy to our fathers, and to remember his holy covenant…

Luke 22:20 And likewise the cup after supper, saying, "This cup which is poured out for you is the new covenant in my blood."

Acts 3:25 You are the sons of the prophets and of the covenant which God gave to your fathers, saying to Abraham, 'And in your posterity shall all the families of the earth be blessed.'

(New American Bible) You are the children of the prophets and of the covenant that God made with your ancestors when he said to Abraham, 'In your offspring all the families of the earth shall be blessed.'

Hebrews 9:15 Therefore he is the mediator of a new covenant, so that those who are called may receive the promised eternal inheritance, since death has occurred which redeems them from the transgressions under the first covenant.

Hebrews 10:16 "This is the covenant that I will make with them after those days, says the Lord: "I will put my laws on their hearts, and write them on their minds."

RESOURCE READING LIST

- Arnold, Eberhard, "Why We Live In Community", Plough Publishing House, 1967
- Christenson, Larry, The Christian Family, Bethany Fellowship, 1970
- Clark, Stephen B., Building Christian Communities, National Ultreya Publications, 1972
- Clark, Stephen B., Building Christian Communities: Strategy for Renewing the Church, Ave Maria Press, 1972
- Clark, Stephen B., Man and Woman in Christ, Tabor House, 1980
- Clark, Stephen B., Patterns of Christian Community, Servant Books, 1984
- Clark, Stephen B., Unordained Elders and Renewal Communities, Paulist Press, 1976
- Delespesse, Max, The Church Community: Leaven & Life-Style, Ave Maria Press, 1973
- Driver, John, Community and Commitment, Herald Press, 1973
- Dubay, Thomas, S.M., Caring: A Biblical Theology of Community, Dimension Books, 1973
- Fitzgerald, George R., Communes: Their Goals, Hopes, Problems, Paulist Press, 1971
- Hinnebusch, Paul, O.P., Community in the Lord, Ave Maria

Press, 1975

– Hinnebusch, Paul, O.P., Friendship in The Lord, Ave Maria Press, 1974

– Jackson, Dave, Coming Together, Bethany Fellowship Inc., 1978

– Jackson, Dave & Neta, Living Together in a World Falling Apart, Creation House, 1974

– Meisel, Anthony C. & del Mastro, M.L., The Rule of St. Benedict, Image Books, 1975

– Miller, Hal, Christian Community Biblical or Optional?, Servant Books, 1979

– Orsy, Ladislas M., Probing the Spirit, Dimension Books, 1976

– Vanier, Jean, Community & Growth: Our Pilgrimage Together, Paulist Press, 1979

– Winter, Michael, Blueprint for a Working Church, Abbey Press, 1973

– Zablocki, Benjamin, The Joyful Community, Penguin Books Inc., 1973

Appendix H:
THE PEOPLE OF GOD: A SNAPSHOT

General: The People of God, Pittsburgh, Pennsylvania, was founded in 1973 and is a full member of the Sword of the Spirit, North American Region.

Membership: At the time of this writing, we have about 200 adults and children. We are ecumenical by intention, even though we have a large number of Catholic members. We have worked and sponsored events among various denominations.

Retreats: We have a cycle of four retreats each year. The Men's, Women's, and University retreats are open and the fourth, our Community Retreat, is for the Community members and invited guests.

Summer Camp: We sponsor a yearly summer camp for fourth, fifth, and sixth-graders, with over 90 campers. This camp serves multiple Sword of the Spirit communities in the Eastern part of the United States. and Eastern Canada. Summer Camp season is a joyful one in the People of God!

Campout: Each summer we sponsor an open campout for adults and children, and we have had guests from neighboring States. We enjoy campfires, fishing, swimming, games and celebrating the Lord's Day.

University Christian Outreach: We have a chapter of University Christian Outreach that is based on the campus of the University of Pittsburgh. It is an ecumenical outreach which helps support students while they remain connected to their denominations.

Koinonia: Our post-University Christian Outreach (ages 22-32) group serves as initiations and discipleship for young adults, both married and single, as they transition from the campus to community life. Monthly Lord's Day celebrations enrich their social life together.

Youth: Our high school age children have regularly attended the "Youth Equipped to Stand" (YES) retreat, and have participated in mission trips, summer internships, and GAP years (service) in the Region. Despite the busy schedules of most high-schoolers, we try to gather them in our high-school program for teaching and fellowship.

Activities and Outreach: We regularly sponsor events such as healing weeks, men's breakfasts, women's fellowship events, and airport caroling. Once or twice a year the leadership invites guest speakers (Charles Simpson, Bob Mumford, etc.) to headline an ecumenical prayer meeting. We have had healing conferences with healing ministers from various parts of the globe.

Community Building: A set of our members have been active in supporting and assisting community building efforts in other parts of the Region. We have assisted with both visitation teams and leadership assistance.

Local Churches: Most of our members are actively involved in their parishes and local congregations. We have attended and supported local church events.

www.ingramcontent.com/pod-product-compliance
Lightning Source LLC
LaVergne TN
LVHW051559070426
835507LV00021B/2670